RACISM Revolves Like A Merry Go 'round: 'round 'n 'round it goes

Dempsey J. Travis

Urban Research Press, Inc.

Prologue By

Dr. Carl C. Bell, M.D., F.A.P.A.
Professor of Clinical Psychiatry
University of Illinois School of Medicine

Urban Research Press, Inc.

Copyright© 1998 Urban Research Press, Inc.
840 East 87th Street, Chicago, Illinois 60619 U.S.A.
· Printed in the United States of America
First Edition
ISBN: 0-941484-27-0
Library of Congress Catalog: 97-061980

Library of Congress Cataloging-in-Publication Data.

Other Urban Research Press Best Sellers by Dempsey J. Travis

PROLOGUE

Dempsey J. Travis has done it again! He has provided us with another outstanding book that delineates the impact of racism on African-Americans. Through the stories in this text, Mr. Travis tells us how African-Americans overcame the problems of racism and discrimination while on their way to developing successful careers. These accounts not only illustrate the dreams of African-American men and women, but also provide the road maps that help the dreams come true.

In this tome, Mr. Travis makes it clear that middle-class status and resources do not protect African-Americans from overt discrimination. He exposes the realities of how racism manifests, even against a black attorney in the federal civil service system or, as in William Cousins' situation, the United States military. However, by using Roma Jones Stewart and William Cousin's conte, Mr. Travis also exemplifies the middle-class African-Americans' recent ability to act forcefully against discrimination. Further, the narrative on Anita Taylor illustrates, while there are some restraints on hostile behavior in public places, African-Americans are more subject to hostility and mistreatment when they venture into places where Whites question their presence. The recapitulations provided by the late Jewel Rogers Lafontant highlight time and energy-consuming aspects of publicly confronting discrimination. In addition, Linda C. Chatman's trials and tribulations underscore how African-Americans may be harmed when they decide to fight against the disrespect they are shown in white businesses. Further, the anecdote on Walter Clark underscores how African-Americans must continually strive to accurately assess Whites in their environment and then decide an appropriate response.

In an interesting chapter that focuses on several great jazz geniuses, Mr. Travis points out that not even creative genius prevents assault from toxic white racism. The horrible, degrading experiences inflicted on African-American entertainers during the first half of this century will lead the reader to marvel at why such noxious ordeals did not kill the birth of jazz within the United States. This section also typifies the inner strength that black folk possess which helps us to overcome adversity and still have an ingenious spirit.

The trials and tribulations that African-Americans experience in corporate America are beautifully profiled in the vignettes that Mr. Travis has collected from the hard working group of middle class, successful, talented African-Americans he has interviewed. The constant pressure to adapt to the values and mores of the white world is unmistakable in the tale of Wendell Campbell. Roma Jones Stewart's story clearly represents the stereotypes Whites may harbor that cause them to think Blacks are a poor employment risk or unable to do the job. Further, it illustrates the discrimination faced on entry into the job market. Bill Bonaparte Jr.'s chronicle embodies the problem of African-American exclusion from white networks. Such restrictions result in an absence of grooming by mentors and a dearth of education from the informal social learning that occurs in business. His sketch also emphasizes the major employment barriers this exclusion creates.

The tokenism experienced by pioneer African-Americans in white-collar positions is poignantly illustrated.

Punishment that many African-Americans risk when they step out of the invisible place that they occupy in corporate settings is depicted in the sojourn of Octavia Harriston. Marginalization happens when black employees in corporate settings find themselves tracked into ghetto jobs with low company job mobility such as the EEOC department, personnel, and community affairs. Failure of the white world and workplace to adapt to Black interests or values, with blacks expected to assimilate into the white culture, is intensely portrayed by Anita Taylor. Clemente Bryson's excursion demonstrates how a support network of brothers and sisters can help an African-American man with a good sense of self maintain his perspective in the white world.

In the tale of Roma Jones Stewart and Dr. Stepto, Mr.Travis emphasizes how, by acting on racist prejudices and assumptions, supervisors and co-workers often create a hostile workplace environment that can contribute to poor performance and failure. The challenge of making alliances with co-workers to achieve that opportunity for a harmonious work place is presented in these vignettes. The difficulty that African-Americans have dealing with white customers and clients who discriminate due to their refusal to put themselves in a subordinate position to a black service provider is powerfully illustrated in Ralph Moore's odyssey of becoming a successful black accountant. Issues of black women being simply tolerated in the workplace, or devalued as sex objects while receiving lower salaries than men is reviewed in the story of Octavia Harriston.

Chapters on Clemente Bryson and Dr. Stepto reveal how African-American entrepreneurs and independent professionals are subjected to many discriminatory practices. Such tactics include exclusion from professional networks, denial of credit, and business location restriction. Stricter rules requirement in judging African-American business is underscored. Dr. Stepto and Roma Jones Stewart's chapters divulge how professions such as the medical and legal professions are still very segregated with Attorney Stewart's account uncovering how even attorneys may face discrimination. Parallels are drawn between African-American entrepreneurs and those pursuing careers in white corporate America. It is noted that a black business person pays a high psychological price for admission into the white business world.

The dilemma of African-American youth attending poorly resourced African-American schools that may provide more social support verses going to a well-resourced White school where they may encounter racial hostility is clearly illustrated in my own story and Buck Brown's experiences at Tilden and Englewood. Dr. Stepto's passage into the white academic world illuminates the impact the decisions white teachers and counselors can have on an African-American student's career. In a white university setting black students may be pressured to give up their identities. African-American college students may be pushed to adopt the surrounding white culture with white middle class styles of talking, dressing, and acting - becoming in essence "Afro-Axons." Norma Jones' narrative demonstrates how African-Americans in white cultural environments frequently develop feelings of alienation and misery as most activities on predominately white campuses reflect white student and faculty interests and traditions.

R. Eugene Pincham's student days at Northwestern University portray how academic institutional culture can become obstacles for African-American scholars. Unfortunately, such institutions have not analyzed the difficulties black students attending white colleges face as a result, such issues have often been ignored by the faculty and administrators. Dr. Stepto's efforts at establishing himself in white academic circles reveal how some white professors question the "competence and potential of black students" based on their stereotypic notions of African-American abilities. Fortunately, since I went to an all black medical school, I did not suffer from a lack of mentors that came from the African-American world. I received as much or more nurturing as white students obtained in a white university, and that would not have been the case had I been accepted to the University of Illinois. Unlike black students at white universities, I got a great deal of feedback from my professors regarding my performance. I never had a sense of being unwanted that I felt at the undergraduate level - an experience which Dr. Stepto suffered firsthand. Further, I could avoid the core precepts of most predominately white colleges that have Euro-American bias in courses, curricula, and research agendas.

This book teaches and re-teaches important lessons about the long lasting impact of slavery and lingering effects noticeable in today's African-American population. Richard Hunt's account exhibits how African-Americans rely on education to lift themselves up from poverty and the importance of having a social support network. It also reveals how by "sticking to it" and having a "by any means necessary" philosophy African-Americans caught in the American caste system can overcome the circumstances of their birth. The importance of instilling a work ethic early in a child's life is accented. Further, it illustrates how "starting at the bottom" is actually a great opportunity to learn a job, thereby developing a strong foundation for further advancement. The book exposes the fact that despite setting a singular goal and failing, you can still soar to unimaginable heights. The tome elucidates that by holding on to your dream you can still win even when the deck is stacked against you. The message is clear - superior skill gets respect despite the lingering racist attitudes that prevail in the U.S., and you can succeed despite adversity. This lesson is clearly illustrated in "Buck" Brown's journey to become an internationally renowned cartoonist. The important lesson of support obtained from the extended family in our lives which drives us to do well is repeated in several chapters. These are inspiring stories of talent and hard work.

In the Epilogue, Mr. Travis brings us back with a hard hitting assessment of where we are in 1997, and how, regarding race relations, it is beginning to feel a lot like 1947.

Dr. Carl C. Bell, M.D., F.A.P.A.

President/CEO Community Mental Health Council
Professor of Clinical Psychiatry,
University of Illinois School of Medicine
Professor of Public Health,
University of Illinois School of Public Health

Dedication

This work is dedicated to the millions of Africans who perished during the crossing of the "Middle Passage" and beyond on the shores of the Americas.

Acknowledgements

This work would not have met it's publication deadline without the talents of Mr. Kitti, the book designer and our Corporate C.P.A. for 25 years. He stepped in and filled the shoes of several soldiers who dropped out of the line of march along the way. Another unexpected find was Jewell E. Diemer who stepped out of her assigned role as our electronic coordinator and doubled in brass as the in-house editor. Her performance was superb. Our senior researcher, Ruby Davis has not lost a step in her search for excellence in fifteen years. I owe a special thanks to Dr. Carl C. Bell, M.D. who read every page of this work and shared his thoughts on the contents in his prologue. Buck Brown has raised art to another level with his ingenious ability to capture the germ of the narratives with caricatures.

I must also extend my thanks and gratitude to the strangers and friends who shared their thoughts in their interviews with me. This work would not have been possible without their cooperation.

Last but equally important was Moselynne E. Travis, my wife and motivator.

Contents

Chapter 19

Epilogue

Bibliography

Index

Ralph Moore aced the C.P.A. exams with the same proficiency he had displayed on the billiards table at the Church Street Pool Hall in Evanston, Illinois.

CHAPTER 1

"Son, Those White Folks Are Just As Good As You"

Ralph Moore was born in 1949 at the Evanston Community Hospital in Evanston, Illinois, which was then the only medical facility in the area that would serve Negro people. The health facility was founded in the home of Dr. Ralph A. Penn by Dr. Isabelle Garnett, the first Negro woman to graduate from the University of Illinois Medical School in 1901, along with her husband Dr. Arthur Butler, a Northwestern University Medical School graduate who joined her in the venture.

In 1938, while an undergraduate scholarship student at Northwestern University, Dr. Robert Stepto of Chicago worked as an orderly at Evanston Community Hospital. Stepto was paid $3.05 a week and thought it was a good deal because they gave him three meals a day and a sleeping room rent-free. No housing accommodations were available

2

for Negro students on the Northwestern University campus, although there were 15 Negro students registered, including Bernard Jefferson, the all star running back in 1937-38, and Helen Payne, who later became a prominent Chicago physician. All students of color commuted on the Howard Street elevated train to their homes on the South Side of Chicago or lived with their family or friends in Evanston.

The initial Negro population in Evanston resulted from a recruitment program for domestic servants that began in the late 1860's. According to the 1870 census, there were 43 Negroes living in the North Shore city and by 1880 there were 129.

Although Ralph Moore was born in Evanston, his father, William Moore, first saw the light of day in 1900 in Louisville, Mississippi, a town 80 miles north of Jackson. The elder Moore spent the first 15 years of his life on a plantation where the white owners controlled the stores, the schools, the Baptist church and the people. The white establishment believed that educating a Negro was un-American. At age 7, little Billy Moore was taken out of the plantation school, a one-room unpainted frame building with the standard outhouse relief station and was put to work on a sun-up to sun-down detail carrying buckets of cool well water and a dipper to cotton pickers working in the sun drenched field.

At age 15, the antebellum environment had embittered him to the point that he left his family's "shot-gun" shack in the middle of a moonless night wearing his Sunday-go-to-meeting overalls and carrying $2.75 in coins in a vest-pocket size, Bull Durham tobacco sack.

The teenager stole a ride on a slow-moving, northbound freight train and prayed all the way that he would not be caught by railroad detectives before he reached the Mason-Dixon line. His first stop north of the Mason-Dixon line was Cleveland, Ohio, where he lived for the next 17 years before coming to Chicago in search of employment during President Herbert Hoover's economic depression.

William Moore met Alberta Cunningham, a 24-year old fellow Mississippian in 1940. They married in 1942, and rented a single room in a kitchenette apartment building in the 4200 block on South Parkway (Dr. Martin Luther King Drive) where they shared the kitchen and bathroom with several families. They lived on South Parkway until 1944 when their first child William Jr. was born. In 1947, they moved to Evanston where Mrs. Moore had worked as a live-in domestic prior to her marriage.

Before coming to Chicago in 1938, Mrs. Moore had picked cotton in Weir, Mississippi, the town where her father had been born into slavery in 1859. Unlike her husband's folks, her family sharecropped for a benevolent plantation owner who permitted her between cotton crops, to finish high school. The school was controlled by the plantation owners. She continued doing domestic work following her marriage until 1957 when she got a job at the Chicago Main Post Office. She worked there until she retired in 1977.

William Moore worked nights for the Illinois Central Railroad until he died in 1964. The intensity of domestic work and caring for two very active teenage sons had wrenched all of the supportive spirit out of Mother Moore's body. She was a very positive lady, but also very tired, too tired to be of any assistance to her sons with their school assignments. Ralph and his older brother William navigated their own way through their high school years with almost no direction from home.

When Ralph was 16 years old, he created his own motivational image and became "Rookie of the Year" at the Church Street pool hall. Mr. Charles Thomas, a history teacher at Evanston Township High School declared: *"Ralph, you are a bum because you are hanging out with the wrong people and not applying yourself in the classroom."*

It took several weeks for Ralph to buy into the "bum" image that Mr. Thomas had planted in his head. In retrospect, he recognized that Charles Thomas was his first positive, professional, Black male role model. Ralph Moore was an angry, misguided teenager, but before he reached adulthood he learned how to channel his dark rage into positive activities.

Ralph stumbled through high school without ever really applying himself. Managing to flunk his first accounting course, he was number 576 out of a graduating class of 900. As a student in the lower two-thirds of his class, Ralph was advised to go to trade school because he really was not college material. Moreover, the counselor said it would be a waste of money and energy for him to even try to go to a four-year university. This was the script that white counselors regularly poured into the ears of the black students at Evanston Township High School. In fairness, it must be said that Evanston Township High did not stand alone in that column.

In spite of Ralph's high school academic record, he spiritually knew that he was college material and fortunately for him, Southern Illinois University at Carbondale, gave him the opportunity to prove it. He believes that the best move he made in his first quarter at the school was joining Kappa Alpha Psi fraternity. The brothers taught him how to study and organize material. As a Kappa pledge, Moore was obligated to spend four hours each night from 6 to 10 p.m., Sunday through Thursday, in the university library.

It was during his college years that he recognized the tremendous sacrifice his mother was making to send him to school. In high school he did not understand the economics of education because it was all taxpayers' money. But when he started to receive those checks his widowed mother sent him to make his education a reality, he realized that he could not waste her money and destroy their dream.

Constantly flashing through Ralph's mind downstate in Carbondale was a vivid image of his mother in Evanston, signing those hard-earned checks for his quarterly tuition. At the same time, the Kappa Alpha Psi big brothers were pushing him toward academic excellence. Those two forces spurred Ralph into making the dean's list for his last 10 quarters. The question that still haunts him today is: What could he have accomplished had he applied himself in high school?

His credible academic achievements were reflected in job offers from 6 of the Big Eight accounting firms. Moore accepted an offer from the Arthur Andersen firm in 1971, although several firms offered more money. Ralph Moore was impressed that Dave Kelly, one of the first Black partners in the Andersen firm, interviewed him. Kelly's presence made Moore feel that the Andersen firm was serious about letting Blacks move up the corporate ladder.

Upward mobility was a concern of Moore's. Being a practical person, he knew he could not make it going to the office wearing an African dashiki and sunglasses. On the other hand, there were some things in his culture that he could not suppress. He pled guilty to not being a Buppie or a button-down, white collar black.

The first day on the job, Moore and several other new hires were invited to lunch by the partner in charge of personnel. As they walked to the Union League Club, they passed a construction site being picketed by Rev. Jesse Jackson and some members of his Operation PUSH organization. Ralph asked the luncheon host how he would feel about his joining the picket line. The partner gasped, *"Oh, my God, have we made another mistake?"* Over lunch the partner regained his composure and said, *"We want you to be socially active, but not in that kind of civil-rights activity."*

The undertone of the rest of the conversation implied that the partner wanted Ralph to be one of those nice conservative Blacks who deep down inside really wanted to be white.

Three months later, Moore was called into the office by one of the senior partners who said, *"We are concerned because we noticed that all the new Black staff members go to lunch together. We want them to assimilate with the rest of the crew."*

Ralph retorted, *"For the past 50 years, all the white guys went to lunch together and that was not unusual. Now that you have 10 Black guys out of 1,000 on the staff, you think some sort of racial evolution is going to take place. People go to lunch with others, black or white, that they are comfortable with."*

Moore was the second Black whom Arthur Andersen Company assigned to its small business division. Preceding Moore was James Williams, a graduate of Tennessee State University and present owner of his own CPA firm. The Andersen people assigned Williams to churches, non-profit organizations and other dead end tasks.

Twenty-two year old, streetwise Ralph Moore refused to accept churches and other non-profit assignments. He argued against those tasks because he rightly felt that when it came time for promotions, they would tell him he lacked the relevant bottom-line, profit-making experience necessary to move up to the next level. His supervisor agreed with that assessment and put him in the company closet for six months where he had plenty of time to count his fingers and toes. Everybody else who had started with him at Arthur Andersen were on assignments gaining experience.

When Ralph got tired of being in exile, he went to his boss, Robert Henry and asked, *"Why haven't I been given a for profit assignment?"* Henry replied, *"We have never sent a Black person to audit one of our small-business clients. Jim Williams, your predecessor, was very satisfied with auditing non-profit institutions. I am afraid to send you out there because we have a lot of clients in Northern Indiana who have never had a Black person work for them. I don't want you to get your feelings hurt."*

Ralph responded, *"I appreciate your concern but I have been Black for a long time. I know what I am facing. As a matter of fact, I knew what obstacles I would be confronted with when I came here. I am not going out there to burn anybody's business down in protest."*

Ralph's stand-up statement was modified by something his mother told him when he was a teenager. She said,

" Son, those white folks are just as good as you are."

Ralph took the Illinois State Certified Public Accountant examination while at the Arthur Andersen firm. He indeed proved that he was qualified and was not there because of some quota system. Young Moore passed the CPA examination in 1973 the first time he sat for it, he was the 68th Negro to pass the test in Illinois. Reaction among many of the white staff people was disbelief because some white employees with MBA degrees from Northwestern, Harvard and the University of Illinois had flunked.

Respect for Ralph Moore's competence went up four-fold. He was transferred to a larger division where he got opportunities to audit some Fortune 500 companies, including the Walgreens Company.

High profile assignments gave Ralph opportunities to meet on a regular basis with some of the high six-figure partners. There he met Leonard Spachek, a managing partner at Arthur Andersen. Ralph mentioned the fact that his mother's sister, Virginia Cunningham, had been Arthur Andersen's live-in maid from 1936 until Andersen's death in 1947. Spachek, after a moment of reflection, said, *"Oh yeah, Ginny, I used to see her all the time when I visited Arthur. This is truly amazing that you are Ginny's nephew and look how far you have come."*

Ralph Moore's aunt scrubbed the toilets and kitchen on her knees for Arthur Andersen and Ralph had become a member of Andersen's professional staff. Through the eyes of white folk, Ralph had come a long way. Thank God, the young man realized that he still had a long way to go. Spachek, the general partner, was making a half million dollars annually in the 1970's.

In 1979, Ralph Moore started his own business. The Arthur Andersen people had taught him how to be professional. His first office was in his apartment where he would get up at 6:30 every morning, except Sunday, take a shower, put on a dark blue suit, white shirt and a power tie. Then he would walk into the next room, sit down at a small desk and hope the phone would ring. He was dressed for success.

Between leaving Arthur Andersen in 1973 and starting his own shop in 1979, Moore held several jobs. The first one was with the Chicago Board of Trade, which was beginning to audit members' accounts. His assignment was to visit offices of commodity brokers and audit their capital accounts and also ascertain whether they were co-mingling monies.

It was in this auditing job that he saw the raw arrogance of racism. The first company he visited would not permit him to go beyond the reception area. He was told that they did not care if he worked for God, they were not going to let a Black audit their books.

On eight separate occasions within a three-week period, he had to call back to the Chicago Board of Trade office to have a white person from the staff come and verify that he worked for the Board.

Ralph was at C.B.O.T. only six weeks when he realized that he had made a big mistake in accepting the position. He found it demeaning to have to physically deliver a white man from the Board of Trade to verify to another white man that he was authorized to audit the books of a member firm. This dehumanizing experience was dumped on him despite his freshly pressed blue suit, snow white shirt and power tie, plus the Chicago Board of Trade identification tag. His only sin for not being found acceptable by the trader was not the content of his character but the color of his skin.

Today Ralph Moore is conducting a very successful National Consulting and Accounting practice from his suite of offices in Chicago.

Historical Note: In 1923, Arthur Jewell Wilson became the first black to pass the Certified Public Accountants examination in Illinois. His first position was with the Binga State Bank, the 1st Black owned state bank in the Land of Lincoln.

Which one of you is the defendant?

CHAPTER 2

THE 'RULE OF 3' VOIDS EQUAL EMPLOY-MENT OPPORTUNITY

Roma Jones Stewart, a practicing attorney, was born in 1936 at Provident Hospital, a Chicago institution for Colored people founded in 1891 by Dr. Daniel Hale Williams, the first American, black or white, to successfully perform open heart surgery.

An act·of racism was the direct cause of Roma Jones's becoming a native Chicagoan. Her father, Sidney A. Jones, Jr., wanted to go to school at Case Western Reserve University School of Law in Cleveland, Ohio, but his application was rejected with the written explanation that they did not think a Colored boy could succeed in the practice of law. Young Jones, a native of Sandersville, Georgia, refused to accept that racist myth because he had read numerous articles about successful Negro lawyers, such as Edward H. Wright, Louis B. Anderson and Edward H. Morris in the Chicago Defender, a Colored-owned newspaper delivered across the United States by Pullman porters working out of Chicago. The Chicago Defender stories stimulated young Jones into coming to Chicago where he applied and was accepted at Northwestern University Law School. He was a student there from 1928 until 1931 and graduated as a member of the Order of the Coif, the highest scholastic honor that can be bestowed on law-school graduates.

His daughter, Roma Jones, did her undergraduate studies at Fisk University in Nashville, Tennessee during the civil rights struggle of the 1950's. Fisk was founded in 1866, for Colored students, largely through the efforts of the abolitionist Clinton Bowen Fisk, an abolition leader in both the American Missionary Association of New York and the Western Freedmen's Aid Commission of Cincinnati. The school, initially known as the Fisk School for Freedmen, was chartered in 1867 as Fisk University.

Fisk University as well as Howard University in Washington, D.C., were the co-ed schools of choice for a large segment of middle class, college-bound Negroes during the first six and a half decades of the 20th century. The voices of Dr. Martin Luther King Jr. Supreme Court Justice Thurgood Marshall and Dr. W.E.B. DuBois echoed through the halls of these schools during their many visits to the university campuses. They inspired many of our young civil rights activists including Diane Nash of Chicago and Marion Barry of Itta Bena, Mississippi, he is the current mayor of Washington, D.C.. The messages of intellectual giants such as Dr. King of the Southern Leadership Conference and Thurgood Marshall, legal counsel for the National Association for the Advancement of Colored People, did not escape Roma Jones. She graduated Phi Beta Kappa from Fisk in 1957 and later from the Georgetown University Law Center in the District of Columbia.

Roma Jones Stewart never had a Black Law professor while in law school. As a student it never crossed her mind to question the professor's knowledge of the law. However, when she became a professor she had students who would argue with her about basic case law. She had a white student at Howard University Law School who would interrupt and contradict her in the middle of a lecture. After several episodes of this foolishness Stewart invited the student into her office where she said: *"If you do that again I am going to expose you and your ignorance in front of the whole class.*

That is the kind of thing that Black professors have to put up with every single day. Academia swirls in the most racist environment you could imagine."

After graduating from the universities, and taking a whirl at teaching Ms. Jones discovered that winning the prize for the highest grades in school did not translate into getting a federal Civil Service job based on the highest test score, that is, not if you were Black. A federal agency had expressed (via mail) a great deal of interest in her taking a position. That interest however melted like butter in a hot skillet when Ms. Jones and the personnel official met for a face-to-face interview. Her ethnic background nullified her superior civil service score. She had the option of passing for white as millions of Negroes had who elected to do during the past century. The low percentage of melanin in her skin, would have made such a transition possible without a hitch.

Since no one scored higher than she did on the test, the federal agency applied the "rule of three." In federal, state and municipal civil service positions, the selection supervising officials have the option of selecting from the top three scorers on a given examination. Therefore, if the top person is an ethnic untouchable, they can select from the individuals who scored second or third on the examination. This selection process subverts the merit selection system and permits the "Lords of the Manor" to practice racism in hiring while complying with published standards.

Roads open to subverting merit hiring or affirmative action are unlimited, and working the federal register is a road well traveled. If a preselected person fails to make the highest score on the Civil Service test, officials may simply cancel the vacancy announcement. The excuse, if one is necessary for not filling the announced vacancy could be one of several, including purported budget problems or departmental reorganization.

Another method of subverting affirmative hiring is rewriting the job description so that it fits the individual one wants to hire. If the target person comes in second, the top scorer is offered a job he or she is not likely to accept. For example, an applicant may be offered a job in Miami, although his or her preference is to work in Seattle. To make a bad matter worse, the applicant may be asked to move to the job site within five working days without the benefit of any relocation allowances.

The road to equal opportunity employment is as rocky in the private sector as it is in the public sector. While in law school at Georgetown, Roma Jones Stewart applied for jobs at several white law firms. It was obvious to her that none of the interviewers read her resume past the section that revealed her race. It also became as clear as spring water that none of the firms had any intention of conducting a legitimate interview with a Negro. Therefore, she decided to get off of the job hunting merry-go-round after three interviews because she was totally uncomfortable placing her body on the bench of humiliation.

Her disparagement did not end with the sham interviews. In 1974 as a prosecuting attorney in Washington, she appeared before a judge with a white male criminal client and the judge looked down from the bench and asked, *"Which one of you is the defendant?"* Stewart simply shook her head as she stood there in her best lawyer's suit holding an armful of legal files. She also discovered as a prosecutor that white judges are very reluctant to see a white person as a criminal when there is a Black person in the picture.

On another occasion, Stewart was assigned to prosecute two co-defendants, a Black woman and a white woman.

Each was charged with grand larceny and Stewart recommended that they both be locked up pending trial. The court clerk called the case of the Black woman first. Stewart stood up and declared, *"I recommend detention."* The judge replied, *"She's detained."* There were no arguments and no reason was required, the Black woman was detained. When the white defendant was called up, Stewart again said, *"I recommend detention."* The judge responded, *"I am not going to detain her."* Stewart retorted, *"Judge, this is the co-defendant to the woman you just detained. These two women are partners in crime. They work together."* The judge refused to change his decision after hearing the explanation.

Prosecutor Stewart jumped from her seat at the prosecutor's table and stood in front of the bench and argued her point for 20 minutes. She gave a myriad reasons why the white girl should be locked up. The judge was told that she had a previous police record and was beyond the control of her parents. In addition, she was living in a terrible situation and her past behavior made her a perfect fit under the statute requiring that she be locked up. The judge still refused to lock her up. After the judge left the bench, the white girl's defense lawyer accused Stewart of having a personal vendetta against his client.

Stewart later was assigned a series of drug cases in which the judge refused to lock up white defendants but threw the key away on Black defendants. Stewart contends that the system is structured to incarcerate Black people while it lets white people go free.

In 1979, the big door of opportunity opened for Roma Jones Stewart. President Jimmy Carter appointed her Chicago friend, Patricia Roberts Harris, also a Georgetown Law Center graduate, as Secretary of Health and Human Services. She, in turn, selected Roma Stewart as the department Director of the Office of Civil Rights, where Stewart had a staff of 1,700 and a budget of $85 million to serve 10 regional offices across the United States. With a Washington office staff of more than 500, the agency's function was to enforce the Federal Civil Rights Act in colleges, universities, public schools, hospitals and welfare institutions. It was in her position as the Federal Director of the Office of Civil Rights that Stewart was able to monitor the merit system from the top.

Ms. Stewart recalls that several of her subordinates attempted to subvert Civil Service Commission regulations in order to promote friends. Stewart blocked their moves and indicated that all positions would be filled based on merit. Each time the department management people tried to make an end run around the system, it would be for the benefit of a white person. Under Stewart's strict pattern of merit promotion, the beneficiary could be white or Black or possibly a member of some other ethnic group. Stewart also noted that some Black managers would go beyond the call of duty to protect the civil-service rights of white individuals over Blacks on their watch.

When Roma Jones Stewart left federal employment to enter private law practice in Washington, she became known in the district as one of the top employment-discrimination lawyers. Many Black brothers and sisters would come to her after white lawyers emptied their pockets and messed up their cases. Several times the charity of her heart overcame her business judgment and caused her to take botched up cases and attempt to mend them, a practice she subsequently found to be a mistake.

Stewart never talked attorney fees when she was settling a client's discrimination case. She considered it a conflict of interest because she observed that many settlement agreements only benefitted the lawyer. The plaintiff walked away with a promise and a prayer and the lawyer collected a fee for as much as $30,000 or more with the judge's blessing.

One of Stewart's more challenging discrimination cases involved a Black woman who was hired based on her academic record and experience to work as an assistant professor at the University of Arkansas Medical School. When the new hire showed up at the school, some members of the faculty went totally berserk. Officials swore they did not hire her as an assistant professor but as a lab assistant or instructor. When she insisted on being an assistant professor, they claimed that they did not have office space for her and suggested that she come back the next year. When the Black woman continued to press her case, school authorities denied they had hired her for any position despite the fact that she had a letter of appointment from the school in her possession.

The spurned assistant professor went to a lawyer who immediately filed a lawsuit. Roma Jones Stewart worked with the lawyer, successfully filing a motion for an injunction. This is the only case Stewart can recall where a court granted an injunction and ordered the university to hire the woman as an assistant professor.

Attorney Roma Jones Stewart also took a case against the University of Maryland because it was similar to the Arkansas case. A search committee focused recruitment efforts on a particularly well qualified Black woman professor. She was selected and approved at several levels when suddenly someone with more seniority in the Sociology Department reversed the decision. She was then denied the position.

The rejected Negro professor had a doctorate, did post-graduate work and had many years of experience as a professor at Morgan State. She had written many articles and had two books in prepublication stages. The "Lords" of the Maryland university rejected her by questioning the quality of some of her articles and asserting that neither of her two books had yet been published. The court ruled in this case that federal judges did not understand all of the subtleties of hiring a professor. Thus, the university was able to hire a young white girl fresh out of graduate school with absolutely no experience.

Roma Jones Stewart was relentless. No institution, she

believed, was too big to tackle when a client had reason to believe that he or she was being discriminated against on a job. Such a case arose when a plaintiff, a dynamite, mid-management Black woman, who was passed over four times for a position that was given to a white male who was less qualified. Stewart presented to the court evidence so overwhelming that the judge stopped the presentation in the middle of the trial and asked the supervisor to come forward, be sworn in and take the stand, the judge said *"Why don't you try to give this matter the appearance of fairness? It appears that it never crossed your mind to put this woman in this high management position even though she completely designed the management system for the office and ran the office on a temporary basis with an exceptionally high performance evaluation."* The witness replied, *"No! It never crossed my mind to put that Colored woman in the position of division chief."* Instead of giving the job to someone who earned it, he hired a white male who performed so poorly that they had to recall someone from retirement to teach the new hire how to do the job. However, Stewart prevailed and the court ultimately ruled in her client's favor.

When Roma Jones Stewart returned to Chicago in 1987, she was appointed to head a section of 31 white male lawyers and one Black female attorney in the Illinois Attorney General's office. There were people in the office who did not want her to have a secretary. She had to go to Attorney General Neil F. Hartigan to get permission to hire an executive secretary. Stewart did not find out until six months had passed that none of the white secretaries would speak to Stewart's Black secretary. While Stewart was section head she also recruited a number of Blacks and Hispanics.

When Stewart left the Attorney General's office to enter private practice in downtown Chicago, most of the Black and Hispanics recruited during her watch left within a few months because white lawyers treated them all like dirt.

Today Attorney Roma Jones Stewart is enjoying a very successful practice in Chicago fighting for those who have been disinherited by the system.

The following statistics were released by the Office of Personnel Management in September 1997:
• African Americans are terminated at three times the rate of whites in the federal government.
• Black males have been steadily declining as a total of the federal workforce; from 7.2 percent in 1984 to 6.6 percent in 1994.
• Almost 60 percent of the Blacks in the federal government are in Grade GS-9 and below.
• The average civil service rank for Blacks in federal service is 7.8. The average for whites is 9.8.
• African Americans are disproportionately in positions with smaller growth potential.
• Only 4 of the top 10 growth jobs in the federal government have Black participation rates of 10 percent or more.
• The percentage of African Americans in five of the top 10 declining jobs is more than 25 percent.
• Minorities in general are disproportionately affected by downsizing.
• While minorities are 28 percent of the federal workforce, they were 33 percent of the Reduction in Force (RIF) in 1996.
• African Americans were 16.9 percent of the federal workforce in 1996 and suffered 25 percent of the RIFs.

Historical Note: Lloyd G.Wheeler, was the first person of color to pass the Illinois Bar Examination, he passed it in 1869.

This is Colored Students Day, jump in the pool the water is fine.

CHAPTER 3

RACISM INHIBITED HIS DESIRE TO LEARN HOW TO SWIM

Wendell Campbell, a prominent practicing Chicago architect, was born in East Chicago, Indiana, which is 27 miles east of Chicago, Illinois, on April 27,1927. He was one of six children yielded from a union between Herman William Campbell of Memphis, Tennessee, and Selma Smith of Cincinnati, Ohio. The senior Campbell was a home improvement contractor. His anchor clients were the First National Bank of East Chicago, Indiana, and the East Chicago Improvement Corporation, a real estate subsidiary of the First National Bank. Wendell's father was kept busy around the clock during the economic depression of the 1930's maintaining the hundreds of foreclosed houses that were owned by the bank. The Campbell kids grew up in one of the bank's repossessed homes which was deeded to their dad as partial payment for some of the work he had done.

At age seven, during the summer of 1934, Wendell got

his first job cleaning up wood chips and sawdust around the job site where his dad was working. The following year during school vacation his father taught him how to handle a paintbrush. His initial task was to paint clothes closets. When his father inspected the first closet little Wendell had painted, he discovered that the boy had left as much paint on the oak finished floor as he had applied to the plastered walls. After a slight reprimand and some additional instruction, the lad put newspaper on the floor to eliminate the additional work involved in removing dried paint from the otherwise beautiful floors.

Shortly after his ninth birthday in May, 1936 Wendell's mother was killed in an automobile accident enroute to Cincinnati with his dad, to pick up his maternal grandmother. Following the loss of Mrs. Selma Campbell, his father and maternal grandmother tenderly assumed the responsibility of raising three small boys and three little girls ranging in age from 4 to 12. All of the boys were kept busy working with their dad after school and during summer vacations.

When Wendell entered East Chicago Washington High School at age 14 in September, 1941 he enrolled in industrial arts courses. He excelled in most of the subjects because of the multiple trade experience and the discipline he gained from working with his dad over a period of seven years. During his senior year, he was paid a substitute teacher's wage to instruct several industrial art classes. The World War II military draft had created a critical shortage of manpower.

Although the East Chicago Washington High School population was twenty-five percent Black, Blacks were excluded from any activity that involved skin contact and social mingling. Therefore, they were prohibited from joining the wrestling and dancing classes. They were also excluded from membership in the Latin Club, the Spanish Club, the French Club and also the Drama Club because they all involved social mixing. On the other hand, they were permitted to officially have a Social Committee for Colored

Activities which included organizing a choir, the Paul Robeson Glee Club, a Black senior luncheon, a Black prom and the election of a Black "shadow" class president. The June 1945 official class president was Ardash Daronasty, a white boy.

Young Campbell never learned to swim because his racial pride would not permit him to use the East Chicago Washington High School swimming pool after it had been garbaged up for four days every week by the white students. The school's maintenance crew religiously deleprosized the pool by draining, and sanitizing it within minutes following its once a week use by the Black students on Thursday afternoon.

The Black star athletes on the football, basketball, baseball, and track teams were, by custom, not invited to attend any mixed gender victory celebrations because it would imply social equality.

Three months after graduating from high school as a National Honor Society scholar, Wendell Campbell was drafted into the United States Army. He became U.S. Army dogtag number 45020514 on September 17,1945, thirty-four days after the shooting war had ended in the South Pacific. Wendell had been offered two four-year athletic scholarships because of his prowess in both football and track. The scholarship opportunities were jettison because the East Chicago Local Draft Board thought that a Black boy serving time in America's Jim Crow peace-time Army would benefit him more than a college education.

Battalion Sergeant Major Wendell Campbell's experience in Japan with the 1492nd Combat Engineers was uneventful with the exception of the fact that racism was always center stage. All of the officers in his battalion of Black soldiers were southern whites except the Chaplain who was an African Methodist member of the cloth from New York City.

Campbell was discharged from the Army on January

18,1947 at Fort Sheridan, Illinois, after serving fourteen months of active duty. He immediately enrolled at the East Chicago branch of the University of Indiana using the G.I. Bill of Rights. He studied architecture there one year before transferring to the School of Architecture at the Illinois Institute of Technology in Chicago, Illinois.

Campbell was the sole Black member of his class at the Illinois Institute of Technology. He and William Morrison, an upper classman, were the only two Blacks enrolled in the School of Architecture. Wendell's G.I. Bill expired at the end of his sophomore year. He needed employment to pay tuition so he went job hunting at architectural offices in downtown Chicago. He could not find a single firm that had a Black working for them in any capacity other than janitorial.

After three weeks of pounding the pavement, he decided to visit with some of his former white classmates on the campus of I.I.T.. Upon seeing Campbell their initial question was, *"Where are you working?"* Wendell shrugged his shoulders and said, *"I am not working. I can't find a job, nobody's hiring."*

They retorted in unison like a Greek chorus, *"What do you mean nobody's hiring? A lot of firms in the Loop are hiring architect students. Did you go by Sydney Morris?"*

Campbell replied, *"Yes! I went to Sydney Morris and he was not hiring."*

"That is bull....," one of his classmates snapped back.

Several of Wendell's Jewish classmates went down to Sydney Morris' office and called him a bucket full of invectives. Two days later Wendell got a telephone call from Sam Brenwasser, head of the drafting department at Sydney Morris. Wendell was invited down to their office to show some of his board work.

Brenwasser said, *"I like your drawings and you seem to know quite a bit about detailing and everything else."*

After making those observations Sam Brenwasser left the room and returned about a half hour later and said, *"We*

still don't have any jobs but a group of students and some former
employees came down here a couple of days ago and made us feel
so doggone uncomfortable we have decided to create a job for you.
We are going to put you on the payroll as of now. However, instead
of coming downtown to work, go to the I.I.T. library and read."

After Wendell spent three days at the library he
received another call late one evening from Brenwasser
requesting that he come down to the office and talk to both
he and Sydney. The first words out of Sam's mouth were, *"We*
feel that you can learn more about how architects function in the
office than you would reading a book or magazine. We still don't
have any spots open on the drawing boards. However, we can offer
you a job as an office boy."

"You would be doing odd jobs around the office such as,
ordering blueprints, and running errands," Sam explained.

With his innate, infectious and disarming smile
Wendell said, *"Okay, I will do it."*

They agreed to pay Wendell $1.25 per hour. He knew
he was being shafted because all of his former classmates
with his background started out earning more and working
on the boards. Underpaying Blacks and women has been an
age old tradition. Four decades earlier, in the 1920's Paul
Revere Williams, the 20th Century dean of the Black
Architects was paid only $15.00 per week working as a utility
man for a Los Angeles architectural firm. At the time he was
a registered architect with a degree in the discipline from the
University of Southern California School of Architecture.

Wendell learned a great deal about the firm's operation that first year by not being chained to the drawing
boards. He called himself the invisible man because he could
wander around the office without attracting attention. He
looked over the shoulders of those working on the boards. He
was permitted to listen in on business conversations between
the firm's partners because he was figuratively a fly on the
wall. His duties actually became an extended classroom in
that he could ask pointed questions and get unambiguous

answers.

When it became close to the time for Wendell to go back to school he asked Sam Brenwasser how they planned to handle his tuition.

Sam barked, *"What do you mean?"*

Wendell retorted, *"We had an understanding that when I got ready to go back to I.I.T. the firm would pay my tuition."*

A light bulb went off in Sam's memory bank and he bellowed, *"How much do you think the tuition is going to be?"*

Wendell gave Sam a figure that sounded like bus fare for a month compared to the current I.I.T.'s tuition.

Upon hearing the amount of the tuition fee, Sam's facial expression changed and he threw up both hands as if a dog had bit a chunk out his behind. He then yelled, *"That's a lot of money. I don't know if Sydney will agree to that."*

Sam left Wendell standing in the middle of his office, went next door to talk to Sydney, and when he returned to Wendell he said: *"Sydney thinks that is a lot of money for tuition, however he agreed to give you a slight raise because he felt that you would be able to save enough money to pay your own tuition next year."*

Wendell clinched his teeth and fist to stabilize himself, and uttered in his customary soft velvet tones, *"Sam that is contrary to our agreement. I told you I was going to work a year then I was going back to school. That is my plan and that is what I intend to do."*

"You don't have enough money to pay your tuition. You already told us that, so how can you go back to school?" Sam snapped back.

Wendell did not answer Sam, however, he subsequently gave him two weeks notice.

Wendell then launched his campaign for raising tuition money. His first stop was the office of the dean at I.I.T. He discovered that they had a plan which would permit him to return to school and pay his tuition on an installment plan. His next stop was the United States Main Post Office where they hired him as a temporary postal clerk for the Christmas rush. His daily schedule was as follows: School from 8 a.m to 5 p.m, the post office from 6 p.m to 10 p.m. He would then study at home from 11 p.m until 3 or 4 a.m. He frequently fell asleep at his study table. He would repeat that same cycle for almost a year.

One of the regular postal clerks working in the same section next to Wendell said that Wendell was the first person he had ever seen fall asleep holding a letter in his hand in mid-air.

Physically and mentally the around the clock work, school and study routine was reaching the 'something-has-got-to-give' level. In addition, he was on the verge of being fired from the post office because of excessive absenteeism.

Wendell's architectural sky was falling on his head in bits and pieces when he received a letter from the dean of the Illinois Institute of Technology requesting that he stop by his office between classes on Thursday, which was two days hence. Campbell was anticipating some bad news, but the dean greeted him with good news. The dean said, *"I have a grant that is available from Commonwealth Edison for a minority student and I would like to know if you would be interested. The grant will pay your full tuition."*

There was a moment of silence because Wendell was emotionally choked after hearing such blessed news. He accepted the grant and was also rehired by the Sidney Morris people to work part time on the boards five nights a week. He continued working for the firm until he graduated from Illinois Institute of Technology in January of 1956.

Two weeks after graduating from the Illinois Institute of Technology, Wendell's father called and asked him to come out to East Chicago, Indiana, and talk to some foundation people who were attempting to acquire his home as a parcel of an urban renewal project.

Forty-eight hours after Wendell had negotiated a favorable deal with the foundation officials for his father, he was called by the same people and offered a position as an urban architect-planner. The Purdue Calumet Foundation only had ten people on the staff but they projected that it would grow to more than one hundred within a year because of the projected magnitude of the development.

A high percentage of the families who would be displaced by the urban renewal development were Black. In addition to being the architect-planner, Wendell became the unofficial buffer between the foundation and the Black community. Wendell Campbell worked for the Purdue Calumet Foundation for ten years and developed a reputation as one of the nation's leading experts on urban designs and planning.

In 1966, Wendell Campbell Associates, Inc. became one among a very small number of black owned architectural corporations in the United States. Campbell subsequently became a member of the American Institute of Architects. He recalls that at the first national meeting he attended in New York City in 1969 there were only two other blacks in attendance and they all acted as if they would be in harm's way if they spoke to each other. In 1926, Paul Revere Williams was the first black to be accepted into membership of the American Institute of Architects.

A year prior to Campbell becoming a member of the A.I.A. Whitney M. Young Jr., Executive Director of the National Urban League, was the A.I.A.'s major guest speaker at their national meeting. He took them to task by stating, *"The American Institute of Architects had fostered urban blight with its "thunderous silence" on race relations and it's lack of Black members, it had thereby tightened the "white noose" of racism around the central city..."* His speech spurred the profession and the public. He enabled Blacks to get more than a toe in a door that had only been barely cracked by Paul Revere Williams in 1926.

When the A.I.A. met in Detroit in 1970 the shield of ice that existed between the blacks in 1969 had melted in that they realized that they would not self-destruct if they got to know each other better. The ten blacks in attendance at the convention decided that they would skip one of the afternoon general meetings and hold a Black caucus session at a local member's office. It was in that meeting that the seed for the idea to organize The National Organization of Minority Architects (NOMA) was planted.

The need for a NOMA was necessitated because there was a total absence of any nuts and bolts information discussed at the A.I.A. sessions that was useful to Blacks in the do's and don't stage of running an architectural business. Historically Blacks had been locked out of the front office operations, therefore, they literally had to reinvent the wheel in the process of getting a handle on how to procure contracts from government agencies and pry open doors at local banks for commercial lines of credit.

The learning process was accelerated in September 1972 when minority housing groups such as the National Organization for Minority Architects, the United Mortgage Bankers of America, the National Association of Minority Contractors, and the Congressional Black Caucus held a joint meeting in Washington, D.C. with Housing and Urban Development officials including George Romney, then Secretary of H.U.D..

Wendell Campbell was NOMA's first president and also one of its founding members. The other founding members were William Brown, Leroy Campbell, John Chase, James Dodd, Kenneth Groggs, Nelson Harris, Andrew Heard, Jeh V. Johnson, Robert Nash, Harold Williams, and Bob Wilson.

According to the 1990 census there are 57,000 registered architects in America, of that number only 817 are Black.

You people don't have no labor pains, you just spit them babies out!

CHAPTER 4

HEY! BLACK GIRL, YOU AIN'T NO MARY TYLER MOORE

After Anita Taylor received her Bachelor of Science degree in Marketing from Michigan State she left home harboring the feeling that the world would be her oyster. Vicariously, she had lived her young adult years in the cloudless television world of Mary Tyler Moore. Her dreamland identity was supported by the fact that in her senior year of college she had been recruited by Sears, the world's largest retailer. Like her heroine she believed that in celebration she could throw her hat up in the air higher than Sears Tower, as she merrily jaunted along the sidewalks of Main Street America.

Her first assignment with Sears was at a store located in a suburb of Minneapolis, Minnesota. Sears recruits had to find their own housing accommodation. It was at this point that Anita had to step out of the television tube and discover that in the real world housing accommodations for Black people in majority white communities were non-existing. She found it psychologically almost painful each time a real estate person rejected her application for shelter because of the color of her skin and not her probity.

There were 5 Blacks in a training group of 30 wandering around the streets of suburban Minneapolis like nomads in search of decent housing. The training coordinator, who by chance happened to be a Black man finally intervened in the name of Sears, Roebuck and Company and resolved their dwelling problems. The apartment seeking experience for Anita Taylor was a reality check of what it was like to be Black in the real world.

Anita worked in the Minneapolis store for 3 1/2 years before being promoted to head a department in a new store located in a shopping mall on the outskirts of Des Moines, Iowa. Most of her customers were farm families who lived within a 50-mile radius of the capital city. The experience of an urbane Black woman dealing with rural white folk was tantamount to taking a step back into the gilded age of the 19th Century when there were no Negroes, Blacks, or African-Americans. To those farmers all of Aunt Jemima's children were Colored. Iowa farmers had not heard that Uncle Tom, Little Eva and all of those "nigger" chasing blood hounds were dead.

Anita was the supervisor of an all white staff in the Apparel Department. One young woman in the department was pregnant. In the course of a discussion about babies the young girl said to Anita: *"It would be easy for you to have a baby because you people just spew them out. It won't bother you at all."* (Meaning black women squat down and spit babies out without any pains during labor or delivery.)

Anita Taylor told me: *"The young lady displayed naivete on a grand scale. She was unlike any person I had ever talked to before. To make a bad matter worse she was both sincere and serious. It was incredible. With that level of mentality swirling around me, I began to understand why I was called "nigger" several times a day as I walked down the mall enroute to the coffee shop."*

In addition to race relations it was difficult for Black women to live in Iowa because it was impossible to find pantyhose and makeup in shades that would blend with the variety of hues found among African-Americans. Locating a place to get their hair done was a roller coaster ride to hell. Their respective families resolved the cosmetic and hosiery problem with care packages from Detroit, Chicago and Atlanta.

The mind set in Iowa in the late 1970's and early 1980's was reflected in a Chamber of Commerce Tourist Bulletin, which read: *"...come to Iowa because the Colored population is almost zero..."* The ad was brought to the attention of the national press and was pulled following some outside editorial criticism.

Anita's fellow managers on the floor were visibly upset because a Black woman was in charge of one of the largest departments in the store, they were jaundiced because her apparel shop was located in an area that made her highly visible to the customers. Ms. Taylor would have been noticeable in a crowded room because of the way she talked, walked and dressed, she radiated finesse. In addition she was both beautiful and smart.

It was a very social thing for the Sears department managers to meet after work at a small bar located within walking distance from the mall. Anita and two other Black female managers had been going to this bar on Friday night for about a month when they got word from one of her white associates that the owners of the bar would prefer that they absent themselves from his establishment.

Anita and her friends were too well bred to go any place where they were not wanted. Therefore, they decided to learn to play golf and participate in annual golf outings since that was a big social event among the white corporate folks. In addition to playing the game, it was an excellent way to learn what was going on in the company and also get to know people who might help you get a foot up the corporate ladder.

Since the girls did not know how to play golf they rented a golf cart on their first outing and rode around the course. To their embarrassment they were stopped several times by white male golfers who thought they were club employees selling food and drinks. Following that encounter the girls decided to sign up for golf lessons. They vowed never to be caught on a golf course without a golf club in their hands. Even with golf clubs in hand they were occasionally stopped by white golfers who asked them if they would fetch miscellaneous items from the clubhouse.

The only game that exceeded Golf in popularity was Corporate Politics. The major political players were members of the "Old Boys" network. Like a golfball all the members were white.

The closest that Black males got to becoming a part of the "Old Boys" network at Sears Tower, were seven Black vice-presidents, who have all since disappeared like Cinderella at midnight. Anita's job ceiling was associate buyer, which was the glass ceiling for most Blacks. The glass ceiling and dismissal of Black executives were buttressed by Reaganomics. President Ronald Reagan's administration fostered the initial steps in the dismantling of the Affirmative Action program for women and minorities.

Anita Taylor's last two years at Sears were spent working hard to make what she describes as an inept white manager look good. She did not know he was color blind until he privately told her to sit next to him in buyers meetings and describe the various clothing color schemes that were being presented.

Supporting a boss who was a follower as opposed to a leader was too much sugar for her dime. Therefore, she terminated her service at Sears before they made their move to the new headquarters in Hoffman Estates, which is located in a Northwest suburb of Chicago, Illinois.

After leaving Sears she fell in love and married a very successful Harvard trained physician. To fill her days, she is presently working as a part-time marketing person in an all white Northside real estate firm that is managed by a female friend who was a former Sears executive.

This is News at 5, tell us what happened.

CHAPTER 5

REACH FOR THE SKY IF THE TREE TOP IS YOUR GOAL

On June 12, 1960, Norma Jones graduated in the top 20 percent of her class from the Little Flower High School for Girls in Philadelphia, Pennsylvania. She was offered a scholarship to Immaculate College, as a result of her debating skills which were evident by the large number of trophies on her mantel that she had won for her high school. She chose not to accept the Immaculate College scholarship because she wanted to go to Pennsylvania State University where they offered an excellent program in broadcast communications.

Some of the monies needed to go to the state university were scrapped together by her parents. Her mother was a public school kindergarten teacher and her father worked in the steel mill as a machinist. The big end of the money required for tuition, housing, food and books was fabricated by layers of Pell grants, loans and scholarships from several small community churches.

Norma was accepted at Penn State without a hitch where she pursued a degree in mass communications. Back in the early 1960's it was out of the ordinary to find women, particularly Black women interested in the broadcast end of the communication business.

Dr. Martin Luther King Jr. and the civil rights movement was in overdrive when she reached her final quarter at the university. The King movement buttressed by a 250,000 person Freedom March orchestrated by A. Phillip Randolph and Bayard Rustin in the nation's capitol, generated a big demand by corporate America for college trained Black employees. Norma received a half dozen or more job offers during the recruiting week at her school. She accepted a position with station KWGN-Channel 2 in Denver, Colorado as an on the air news reporter. She was able and more than qualified to shoulder mount the camera and shoot her own footage, which she did while conducting the interview and subsequently developed the film (this was before video), edit it and do the voice over. She was always on schedule for the evening news. Her company business card read news reporter/photographer. Today most television news reporters are accompanied on assignments by a camera crew. From jump street Norma was bucking to become an evening news anchor.

The young woman from the "City of Brotherly Love and Sisterly Affection" was the first professional Black woman to be hired at the Denver station. In addition to her on the air duties, she was a street reporter covering all kinds of events including those at City Hall and the State House.

In keeping with the "Black Is Beautiful" philosophy of the 60's and early 70's, Norma was wearing her hair in a fashionable Afro style similar to the beautiful Angela Davis, the U.C.L.A. philosophy instructor. The studio camera man in a fit of anti-Black rebellion told Norma that he couldn't fit her big Afro hair-do in the camera frame. Her response to his imaginary problem was to fluff her hair into a bigger Afro. She reminded the camera man that she was the morning anchor person and that it was his job to fit her full Afro within the parameter of the screen. At that point she was smiling and laughing at the camera man when she suggested: *"You can accomplish our objective by simply rolling the camera back about two feet."*

During the late 60's and early 70's each one of the television and radio stations in Denver had at least one token Negro. That was also true of the Denver newspapers. The media mirrored corporate America.

Several months after she started working at station KWGN Norma began networking with another Black woman who was employed at station WKOA television in Denver. Her new friend had been recruited from City College of New York. She had been working in the "Mile High" city for just a little over a year when she met Norma. The woman alerted Norma to some of the pitfalls that on the air Blacks had experienced. For example, she warned her not to list her name in the telephone book. The WKOA news reporter explained that prior to changing her telephone number to an unlisted one she was inundated with hate mail and all kinds of racist and kinky telephone calls. As a matter of fact, one of the crank callers was able to get through to her at the television station and blurt out a statement that flustered her just before she was ready to go on the air. In this instance the caller said: *"I can smell your 'nigger' odor through the television set."*

On the other hand, there were many whites at station KWGN who went out of their way to be friendly. They would invite Norma and her husband to their homes. As a matter of fact, they did everything within reason to make the Jones' comfortable and a part of their social activities. Although both of the Jones' had Masters Degrees they could not blend with their white associates beyond shop talk because early conditioning by America's "birth to the grave" separatist society almost guaranteed that they would never have very much in common. This is said knowing that there are a minority of individuals on both sides of the cotton curtain that are not inhibited by racist rules.

Norma and her husband found socializing with white folks an uncomfortable experience. When they went to parties they never had the desire to stay until the end. They usually showed their faces at company functions for a long enough period to make their presence felt and then they quietly dismissed themselves.

Her husband's discomfort around her Channel 2 associates made it difficult for her to play the assimilation game. Mr. Jones would make light cocktail conversation describing his duties as an educator at the gathering whenever he was asked about his work, however he never enjoyed doing it.

Norma learned in talking to the other Black women in the television business that her husband's discomfort with white folks was not unique. It actually caused a psychic strain among some of the husbands when they were dragged by their wives into integrated activities. Whenever they could avoid social functions they did.

After a two year stint Norma left Channel 2 for a higher paying position with the United States Commission on Civil Rights. The agency hired her because of her investigative experience as a reporter. Her first assignment was to investigate the absence of minorities in the media. The agency picked a state that one would not generally think of for an expose; it was Montana. Very few Blacks lived there, however a large number of Native Americans were inhabitants. It was felt by the commission that the Indians should be on television reporting what was going on in their own environment.

A hearing was held and the same arguments that have been historically employed for excluding Blacks from the upper chambers of commerce were being made against the Indians. They argued that the "Red Men" were not prepared, in spite of the fact that many of them had backgrounds in photography, as well as experience in producing high quality videos.

During the hearings, evidence was presented showing that there were a number of Indians studying broadcast communications at the University of Montana. Later a report was issued by the United States Commission on Civil Rights widely circulating the fact that the media practiced racism against Native Americans.

Norma Jones' excellent work with the Commission was brought to the attention of the proper authorities in President Jimmy Carter's Administration and she was appointed Regional Director of Public Affairs for the Department of Health and Human Services. She was euphoric over the appointment.

The four years that she worked as Regional Director went by quickly. Unfortunately, her new job played out like the lyrics of a popular song entitled "That's Life," in that she was riding high in June and cut down in January by the newly elected President Ronald Reagan.

Norma was not prepared to leave her government heaven when she received a telephone call early one morning indicating that President Ronald Reagan was on a patronage hunt and therefore, wanted the resignation of each Carter appointee. The gate to her Camelot was slammed tighter than the doors to the executive John.

The last time I spoke with Norma Jones she reported she had had jobs at Coors in Denver, as manager of the Consumer Information Center and at W.T.T.W. Public Television in Chicago.

Her dream of becoming an evening television anchor had withered like an unplucked grape on a frosted vine.

At the Northwestern Medill School of Journalism, Bryson learned that education was not double dutch.

CHAPTER 6

EDUCATION IS NOT DOUBLE DUTCH

Clemente Bryson was born in Pittsburgh, Pennsylvania on June 4, 1952. His father died of lung cancer at age 34 from an overdose of cigarettes when he was only six years old. Young Bryson was reared by his mother, a public school teacher, and his maternal grandmother.

When he reached fourth grade 5% of the students in the Negro middle school he attended were bussed to the Taylor Allerdice School which was located in Pittsburgh's Squirrel Hill District, a predominantly upper-class Jewish community. The school curriculum at Allerdice was excellent but some members of the faculty treated Negro children like untouchables.

Bryson's fifth grade teacher asked him what he wanted to be when he grew up, he told her he wanted to be a journalist and work for Mr. Robert S. Vann's "Pittsburgh Courier", a Negro owned weekly newspaper, or the "Ebony" magazine which was published by John H. Johnson a Negro entrepreneur in Chicago. She retorted: *"You cannot write well enough to handle fast lane academic courses. Therefore, it is my opinion that you would certainly be more comfortable in an industrial curriculum."*

At dinner Bryson told his mother what the teacher said about his not being smart enough for the academic lane. His mother reacted in a fit of rage upon hearing the teacher's suggestion. Later when she calmed down she told her only child that he had to believe in himself, and by doing so he would be able to achieve whatever his little heart desired.

The next morning Bryson was accompanied to school by his mother, who was simmering with anger. The first thing she said to his teacher after uttering a very crusty good morning was: *"What's the deal here! Why isn't my son in advance studies?"* Before the baffled instructor could reply she asked to see the records of the other students in advance studies. Her request could not be denied because the information she was seeking was public record. It turns out that Bryson's test scores were in the 98 percentile. He had been denied a lane on the fast track not because he was a dullard, but because he was a Negro.

His high school experience mirrored his grammar school nightmare. The school systems usually reflect the thinking of the dominant body of the community unless it happens to be black.

Going from a racist Pittsburgh public school system to Fisk University, a historical Negro institution in Nashville, Tennessee was a real breath of fresh air. It was intellectually exciting to be mentored by Negro teachers who really took time to explain things. They gave him a better perspective of the subjects in that they put new flesh on old intellectual skeletons. In addition they made themselves available for guidance when things were not clearly digestible.

At Fisk, Bryson had an opportunity to intern at WFM-T.V. which owns Nashville's "Grand Ole' Opry". His on the job training included learning to be a reporter, editing and shooting film. Nashville was a small market in which there were no unions thus he really got a wide open opportunity to get a lot of hands-on experience. The University made the work study arrangement with the T.V. studio because they did not have an in-house journalism department for those wishing to study that discipline.

Bryson enjoyed the Nashville environment and was prepared to stay at Fisk beyond the duration. Then out of the clear blue sky a recruiter from Northwestern University came to the Fisk University campus and put on a full court press with an offer of a 100% scholarship to the graduate school of journalism at the Medill School. It was an accelerated 12 month program for the best and the brightest.

The temptation of a free ride was so great, Bryson quit his job at WFM-T.V. and left the comfortable environment of Nashville for the cold wintery winds off Lake Michigan in Evanston, Illinois. His roommate was a rich white boy whose folks lived on Chestnut Street which is located in Chicago's Gold Coast District. The rich kid was a party animal who never studied, yet he maintained a 4.0 grade point average. At the same time, Bryson was catching hell in a special 11 week preparation program because he had not officially studied journalism in undergraduate school. The 11 weeks were a tooth pulling academic grind in that the curriculum managed to cram 4 years of journalism into less than 3 months. It was during this period that the boy from the "Smokey City" realized that education was not double dutch.

In addition to breaking books and sweating bullets every night for 8 to 10 hours Bryson had to make a psychological transition from four years of heavy duty militant blackness at Fisk University to a white world that had never eaten neckbones, chitterlings and cold-water cornbread as a main course meal.

To maintain his sanity and keep his head screwed on right he would make a mad dash off the campus every Saturday morning to spend weekends on the southside of

Chicago with some Fisk graduates and some Kappa Alpha Psi fraternity brothers. Seeing and talking with the brothers and sisters in the hood was the mental nourishment that he needed to sustain himself week after week.

Bryson successfully completed both the 11 week prep program and the 12 month accelerated graduate school as number 5 in his class of 270 with a 3.9 grade point average. In the final quarter before graduation, one of his teachers who was also the vice president of a Chicago television station offered him a job as an assistant field producer. He worked in that capacity for two years without a raise or promotion. Most of the white folks who started with him were being rewarded with important sounding titles and also being mentored and pushed up the corporate ladder.

In disgust Bryson quit the television station after giving proper notice and went back to Northwestern University's Evanston campus during the corporate recruiting period in search of a job opportunity. He was offered and accepted a position with a major advertising agency. When he reported for work at his new gig he was told he would be working as a copy writer. He in turn told his immediate supervisor that he had several years of film production experience and therefore wanted to use his film skills, if it was at all possible. He was told to go upstairs and see the creative director.

The wind was blowing at his back that day because when he met with the creative director who was shooting a spot for the Zenith Corporation at the time, their personalities meshed and he was asked to come aboard after a very brief conversation. He rose rapidly through the ranks and became the youngest Vice-President in the agency at age 30. He had met his own self-imposed 5-year goal. However, over the next 9 years his white contemporaries left him in the dust as they moved up the ladder to higher corporate positions. Bryson was being stepped over and around while his white colleagues became Senior Vice-Presidents with line responsibility.

Although Bryson was an award winning Vice-President he had to continue pushing the envelope. He had to ask to be made Vice-President. He had to request more responsibility. He never got a pay raise without asking for it, whereas perks and authority flowed to his white colleagues automatically.

After 14 years of being bounced off the "Great White Wall" Bryson decided he would reinvent himself and start his own advertising and public relations agency. Six top-notch fellow black employees followed him out of the door and joined him in his new venture. None of the Blacks who left with him had received the kind of recognition that they deserved. On the other hand, the old agency quickly promoted another black to Vice-President to fill the slot that Bryson had created by pushing the envelope. To his knowledge his V.P. successor is still the only Black officer in that world wide agency.

Bryson had not been on his own but a short period of time when he discovered that advertisers look at Black advertising agencies through a different set of bifocals when you are acting on your own behalf instead of carrying water on both shoulders for the man. Advertisers saw Black agencies as an appendage as opposed to a new marketing dimension. The same people who praised Bryson's work yesterday when he was working for "the man" wouldn't even give him an interview today.

According to the best numbers available, today's Black owned advertising agencies control less than 1/2 of 1 percent of the advertising and public relations market. By the year 2000 it could be less because the latest trend in the business is to hire a high profile Black as a point person and publicize it as a merger or subsidiary. Thereby tightening the noose by several notches around the total market.

Although I got E+ in all my subjects, Corporate America failed me.

CHAPTER 7

HER WHITE STUDENTS PASSED BUT THEIR BLACK TEACHER FAILED

In June 1960, Octavia Harriston, moved to Evanston, Illinois from Marion, Alabama which is approximately 30 miles from Selma where Dr. Martin Luther King, Jr. staged his long remembered bloody Selma to Montgomery walk on Sunday March 8, 1964. On that Sunday 650 marchers were attacked and turned back on Selma's Edmund Pettus Bridge by mounted police wielding tear gas, clubs, and bull whips. The assault left 100 Blacks hospitalized and another 70 injured.

Before the civil rights movement had reached its fervor pitch Octavia had been sent North by her parents to live with her maternal grandmother who enrolled her in the Evanston Township High School from which she graduated without fanfare in 1962. Octavia, has been an avid reader since her early childhood and she attributes most of learning to the classics that she read outside of the classrooms. The young lady got married to her Alabama sweetheart a year after finishing her public school education.

Late one morning while enjoying the comforts of being a housewife she read a want ad for a part-time typist position in a major Chicago newspaper. When she inquired about the position she discovered the employer was actually seeking salespeople with typing skills to service advertising inquiries. Although Octavia describes herself as an introverted person with no sales experience she was a top flight 85 words per minute typist. She was hired by the newspaper because of her typing skill.

One day while rambling through some old newspaper files researching information for an advertising client she discovered a number of ads from the yesteryears that read "Jobs For Whites Only" and "No Coloreds Need Apply." The racial labeling of ads was partially discontinued by some urban daily papers in the early 1950's shortly before the dawning of the post-World War II civil rights revolution.

Octavia received a telephone call at the newspaper one morning about 9:15 from a brusque sounding woman with a heavy Eastern European accent. The caller asked Octavia to help her compose an ad for an apartment she wanted to lease in a two-flat building that she owned on the northwest side of Chicago. The lady told Octavia that the ad should read "For Whites Only." Octavia politely told the customer that the newspaper would not print an ad with restrictive ethnic wording.

The woman replied: *"Oh well! I guess if any of them people called I would be able to recognize them by their voices."*

Octavia retorted: *"I doubt very seriously that you would be able to discern them by their voices, because you have been talking to one of them people for the past half hour and you did not have a clue that you were speaking to a Black."*

The customer banged the phone down without saying thank you or good-bye.

The ad writing job had become both tiresome and boring to Octavia after eight years. She had traveled many miles from desk to desk within the department handling real estate ads, automotive ads, help wanted and situation wanted ads. She finally began to entertain the notion that she had reached her employable peak at the newspaper. To make bad matters worse young white girls were being brought into the department fresh out of high school who could not find their way to the toilet with a Triple A road map. Her assignment was to show them the way. In a relatively short period of time she was rudely awakened to find herself reporting to some of her former young students. Ouch! The man certainly knows how to hurt an old hand.

Her cup was full and had runneth over when she finally decided to leave the newspaper and go to work at the University of Chicago as an executive secretary for the director of the hospital's volunteer department. Octavia had not been on the hospital payroll two weeks when she began receiving calls from the new manager at the newspaper asking her to come back to work. Her first response was: *"I am not interested in retreading old tires, plus I like my new job."* That negative response did not stop the manager's calls. He finally got her attention when he offered to pay her $50.00 more per week than she had been making when she left.

Without too much hesitation she said: *"I will accept your offer if you will increase the salary to $75.00 per week with annual increments of not less than $1,500.00."*

The manager snapped back: *"It's a deal."*

There were several moments of thoughtful silence and then she blurted: *"Tell me that I can look forward to promotions based on my ability and performance rather than on the color of my skin."*

He said: *"You got it."*

Without an ounce of hesitation she replied: *"I want to thank you for accepting my counter offer; however, I will not be able to report to your shop without giving the University of Chicago Hospital people the proper two weeks notice."*

Octavia returned to the job saddled with the same old responsibility of wearing a miniature size telephone headset, servicing ad inquiries and counseling clients who needed more than routine assistance. After warming the undersized seat of the chair for another two years she noted that the employer had not kept his promise when he promoted another young white woman over her that she had recently trained. Following that act she was inflamed enough to jump into the murky blue waters of the Chicago River. The action she was about to take was going to put her job at risk at a time when she and her husband were attempting to qualify to buy a house. However, her mind set propelled her into storming across the office to her supervisor's desk and saying, *"I quit."*

The supervisor recoiled, *"What do you mean you quit?"*

Octavia snapped: *"I mean I quit! I have seen a number of white men and women that I have trained advance over me time and time again. I have had it up to the bridge of my nose with these racial slights. I cannot bear the weight this cross of third class citizenship any longer."*

The supervisor's mouth flew open like a trap door, his face turned beet red when he muttered: *"Do you have another job, what are you going to do?"*

Octavia spurted, *"I am going home and be Mrs. Harriston. I may not have as many rings as I would like to have, but I will have a roof over my head, food on my table, and for dessert, I will have peace of mind and self respect."*

When the manager of the department heard the heated conversation between Octavia and her supervisor, he jumped out of his chair, ran out of his office like he was going to a fire without a water hose. He hoped to cool Octavia down by inviting her to have lunch with him in a restaurant outside of the company.

When they returned to the office after lunch following what could have been an exit interview she was promoted to supervisor of the part-time ad takers, most of whom were college students and housewives. In less than a year Octavia was pushed up another rung on the job ladder to supervisor of the help wanted ad division. This division at that time was responsible for adding approximately $40 million a year to the company's bottom line.

Octavia was on the move because in less than a year she was promoted to sales manager for solicitors advertising. This new position was high profile in that she traveled across the state giving slide presentations to potential advertisers on the merits of doing business with her paper. The shy Marion, Alabama girl had become a very gifted, spellbinding speaker. As a matter of fact, she was so good that on one occasion they flew her out of Midway Airport to Palm Springs, California on the company's corporate jet to make a sales presentation to a group of agency people who were currently doing business with the newspaper.

Everything was going along smoothly until she stepped on a broken rung of the corporate ladder. The cause of the break became crystal clear in an article that appeared in the house organ of the company. The company paper listed the names of the Who's Who along with their pictures. Octavia's picture and name were nowhere to be found although she was the sales manager of the department. In her place was the picture of a young white woman that she had trained and mentored. Upon seeing the article and pictures she ran downstairs with her eyes full of tears and confronted the manager who had been responsible for her coming back to the newspaper.

"Why isn't my picture in this article?" she howled with a grimace across her face that would have frightened King Kong.

The manager replied, *"Octavia it's an oversight. We didn't have a picture of you."*

She said: *"I beg your pardon do you think I am a fool? You should know that I know that you have a whole floor full of camera people downstairs, any one of whom could have taken and developed a picture of me in less than ten minutes."*

To appease her and at the same time enlarge the Machiavellian web of deception, they promoted Octavia to the position of Manager of the Equal Employment Opportunity program for the newspaper. She was reluctant about taking the job because there was nothing in her background or training that would indicate that she was qualified. Her formal education ended when she graduated from the Evanston Township High School in Evanston, Illinois. On the other hand, she was a lifelong cafeteria reader.

Her reservation about accepting the new assignment was overridden by the vice-president of personnel who said, *"Octavia I don't remember half the things I learned in college. Furthermore, some of the biggest fools I ever met were college educated. I want you for that position. I will train you for it."*

Octavia was still not convinced because she knew how she would feel if someone without personnel experience or college training took a job for which she was qualified and had salivated to get. She would hate them with the same intensity that most southerners hated the northern carpet-baggers following the Civil War.

In January 1985, Octavia officially became the company's recruiter, that is for every department except editorial. The editorial people said they would do their own recruiting because she was not qualified to identify good writers. The company's advertising department closed the door in her face, claiming that they had someone within the department to do their recruiting.

Before the E.E.O. Managerial position went into a tail-spin the Vice-President of Human Resources intervened and gave Octavia some new directions. He said: *"I want you to go down south to some of those historical Negro colleges like Florida A & M, Howard University, Fisk and Morehouse and talk to some of those bright students contemplating graduation in the next class to consider coming to work with us."*

The company's Equal Employment Opportunity Manager's job description became that of a Negro job recruiter.

The odyssey of Octavia Harriston does not have a happy ending because she has filed a lawsuit against her former employer for several million dollars alleging racial discrimination and harassment.

I am going to humble this wireless monster.

CHAPTER 8

THE BONAPARTE CONNECTION INC.

William Bonaparte, Jr. was born on December 11, 1942 in Chicago at the Cook County Hospital on West Harrison Street. His parents lived in a public housing development known as Princeton Park on the South Side of the city.

He received his primary education at Gillespie Elementary School at 94th and State Street. After graduating from grammar school he attended Calumet High for a semester and then transferred to the newly built Harlan High School for Blacks in the West Chesterfield Community. This double transferring took place during a period in 1959 when the Superintendent of Public Schools Benjamin C. Willis was hell bent and working overtime to keep Chicago's Public Schools segregated.

Following high school, he had the very good fortune of getting a job as an apprentice printer. He held that position until he was drafted into the military service for a two year hitch.

In August 1963 at the age of 21 the only grind that Bill Bonaparte Jr. could find after serving in the United States Army was his old one where they gave him credit for the period he was in uniform. His new status on the job was that of a journeyman printer at the Tabulating Card Company located at 63rd and Narragansett Avenue on the southwest side of Chicago.

When he was drafted into the service in 1961 he scored 147 on the I.Q. test. A 147 intelligence quotient is seven points above the genius base level which is 140. The Army's qualifying entry I.Q. score in early 1997 was only 95 and there was a debate about lowering that score to 90 in order to meet a projected recruiting quota.

Young Bonaparte's extraordinary intellect and cool temperament did not escape the attention of Al Raby, a former Chicago public school teacher and Dr. Martin Luther King's civil rights counterpart in Chicago. In the summer and fall of 1963, Raby was demonstrating against utility companies for job opportunities. He was recruiting young, smart, cool headed, non-violent individuals to join him in demonstration protests, street sitdown strikes and daily freedom marches. Bonaparte stepped forward and volunteered to march for Freedom Now.

During the summer of 1965 Al Raby and his marchers would assemble daily at Buckingham Fountain in Grant Park at 12:30 p.m. and march for Freedom Now. Their destination would depend upon the issue of the day. For a period of time that summer Dick Gregory the comedian and civil rights activist commuted daily from San Francisco to Chicago to participate in those marches.

The Illinois Bell Telephone Company was among the first utility companies to participate in a program that allowed Negroes to take their placement test. Bonaparte was among a select group that sat for the examination. He passed the test and was offered a job as an elevator operator, which he did not accept. Several decades earlier Illinois Bell Telephone Company had pioneered in white collar employment by hiring some Black women as switchboard operators, in addition to coin box collectors and male custodians. There were several Blacks working at the managerial level in Illinois Bell's branch offices in the Black community.

After turning down the position of elevator operator Bonaparte subsequently received a notice from Illinois Bell indicating that he had been placed on a waiting list to become a P.B.X. installer. He did not know what it meant, and did not care. All he wanted was a good paying job. Every morning he would call the gentleman at the employment office to find out what his number was on the P.B.X. waiting list. As a matter of fact on several occasions he called the placement office three times in a single day. Finally, he received a letter requesting that he come into the employment office for a second interview. He was told after they carefully reviewed his application and test papers that he was being hired as a P.B.X. apprentice.

The interviewer congratulated Bonaparte on being hired and then commenced to tell him a number of job related horror stories. He was told that his first obstacle was to join the International Brotherhood of Electrical Workers Union #134. A union that historically had never accepted a person of color as a member. Once he succeeded in breaking that barrier with the assistance of the Illinois Bell Telephone Company he was told by a local union official that they could not predict how the other white union tradesmen would react to working with him in the field.

Although Bonaparte as a minority of one had many reasons to be concerned about coming in harm's way, he was willing to take those chances. In so doing, he became the first Black member of the Electrical Worker's Union and the first Black apprentice P.B.X. installer for Illinois Bell. The company did not hire another Black P.B.X. apprentice until five years after Bonaparte entered the program and had become a journeyman.

Bonaparte made the following observation: *The white guys never tried to like me, know me or teach me. They had made up their minds that they did not like "niggers" long before I got there. They did not have to respect me but they had to show deference to the fact that I was a card carrying member of the International Brotherhood of Electrical Workers Union.*

The white boys treated me like I had some kind of contagious disease and they decided to isolate me. They figuratively buried me in the switching room which was off limits to anyone who was not officially assigned to work there. Ordinarily you would have had to have at least 17 years seniority before you got the privilege of working in the switching room. What they considered my punishment for being Black turned out to be the greatest opportunity of my lifetime. I learned to build the line finders, the connectors, and I read all of the blueprints. I even read the small print on all of the component parts of the machines. I was a fox in the hen house in that my job was the guts of the telephone system. The white boys were having fun like grasshoppers playing in the summer sun as they crawled around on the floor pulling cables in the quiet areas of the offices where they could ogle at the legs of the young lily white secretaries.

There were two components to the P.B.X. system, the cable that was connected to the telephones and the switching apparatus which was literally the heartbeat of the system. I spent the four years of my apprenticeship working in the switching room. However, when they let me out I was a tiger with the capability of building a P.B.X. system with my own hands. I did not need to have those white boys hanging on my ankles.

Machinewise I had become sharper than a tack. My first

solo assignment was installing a P.B.X. system for the Bank of America when they moved into one of Chicago's LaSalle Street canyons at 29 South. My immediate boss recognized my capabilities, therefore, he assigned me to get the job done for the California branch bank in the shortest period of time. The engineers had estimated it would take 800 man hours to complete the job. I finished it by my lonesome within 75 hours.

Completing the job in such a short record period of time created a big problem with the union, fellow employees, and some of the middle management bosses. Many of the tradesmen had been gold bricking on the job for years and my feat turned a bright spotlight on their foot dragging work habits. The engineer that made estimates in reference to the number of man hours that would be needed to complete the mission did not come out of the mess smelling like roses. The white boys thought that I would fall flat on my face, but I turned out to be one of Illinois Bell's most productive P.B.X. men during that period.

They began giving me bigger jobs. I was promoted to journeyman within a year after I came off of the initial P.B.X. assignment. I was then made foreman of a K.C.X. gang. After an additional 18 months some of the other tradesmen wanted me to replace Danny Petrowski, who was my boss. When Danny heard the rumor he became mad as hell at me, however he never knew that I personally had never entertained any notion about displacing him.

Bonaparte's skills in the field were making a lot of people uncomfortable, therefore they took him out of the briar patch where he was using his mind and his hands and put him in personnel where he became a paper chaser and manager of the personnel assignment center. He spent a year in that position before they shuttled him back into a K.C.X. engineering position.

His stint in engineering was followed by promoting him to Installation Superintendent for the west side of Chicago. Bonaparte's job movements were reminiscent of Jonathan Swift's Gulliver in Gulliver's Travels in that he was moving across the job map with unusual rapidity. His next advancement was that of wire chief of the Monroe District which geographically covered the area from Halsted on the east and to the west a couple of blocks beyond Western Avenue, the northern boundary of the district was Kinzie and the southern border was 22nd Street.

When Bonaparte walked into the office of his new assignment as wire chief at 1340 West Monroe the stench of racial hatred was so thick you could cut it with a butter knife. Down the street at the company garage at 1 South Loomis the conditions were even worse. The word "nigger" was sprayed all over the walls and ceilings. Bonaparte's heart dropped as he gazed around the facility. He knew that he was in for a barrel full of trouble.

When he called his first meeting in the garage with all of the wire technicians and their bosses he could not get a word in edgewise because the workers were disruptive, rude and loud. They were a motley looking cigarette smoking bunch. Many of them wore graffiti covered t-shirts, loose hanging bell-bottom slacks. Moreover they were unshaven and unkempt. Bonaparte could not get a teaspoonfull of order out of the wild ones, in disgust he recessed the meeting until the following week.

During his second week at the South Loomis Street garage he called another meeting and suspended two of the straw bosses because he considered them to be among the ring leaders of the disorder. His bogart mannerism did not resolve the state of racial discontent.

When Bonaparte called a third meeting the following week he tried a new twist with a fifty dollar bill. Several minutes after he sat down and called the meeting to order he pulled out of his hip pocket an envelope containing a fifty dollar bill which he passed to an Irishman who answered to the name of George O'Hare. George opened the envelope and said:

"What is this for boy?"

Bonaparte replied:

"If you can walk into this garage and still have a job with Illinois Bell 30 days from now, the money is yours."

O'Hare laughed in Bonaparte's face.

Within eighteen days after Bonaparte made the threat he caught O'Hare drinking on three separate occasions in 22nd Street watering holes. The third time he caught him he fired him on the spot. O'Hare had overlooked the obvious and that was, he could camouflage his 180 pound body in a pub but he could not hide the dark green Illinois Bell truck. The union sided with Bonaparte in his actions against O'Hare.

When Bonaparte called his fourth meeting he found a group of workers who were less rowdy, only a few had on t-shirts, ninety percent of them were cleanly shaven, and the racist graffiti on the walls and ceiling had been removed.

As Bonaparte's eyes swiveled across the faces of the men who had assembled in the garage he reached into his pocket and pulled out another envelope containing a $50.00 bill. He passed it back to Gordy Sullivan who was standing at the rear edge of the group. In Bill's black book Gordy was foul mouth #2 in that gang of 40. Ten days after receiving the white envelope Gordy visited Bonaparte's office on West Monroe and handed him the envelope with the $50.00 bill and told him he wanted peace. From that point forward that group of men became members of Illinois Bell's "A" team.

Bonaparte was mentally an Illinois Bell team player, but he was never physically a part of the team. When the other district managers had a drinking and golf party outing in Wisconsin they would always invite the colored boy, but they never gave him the right time. For example, if they were going to tee off at 7a.m. they would tell him 3p.m.. When he arrived they would apologize for giving him the wrong time in spite of the fact that they knew damn well he loved to play golf. On his good days Bill could shoot in the 70's.

He never got information in the same time frame as his white peers. Bill always had to huddle by himself. The job isolation has had a lasting psychological effect on Bill in that the after shock of those early experiences play back like nightmares from time to time.

Reflecting on the past thirty years Bonaparte states: *"No matter what level of success I achieved, I still had to prove over and over that I was competent and trust-worthy."*

Bonaparte's capability placed him on the A.T.& T. side of the employment ledger after the government split up the Bell Telephone System. In February 1985 he received the Keystone Award from AT&T for being among those managers who took risks and won. The award has only been given to 26 individuals in the company's history.

AT&T at that time needed Black visibility in Chicago, a city where Harold Washington had recently been elected as it's first Black mayor. Bonaparte was the man they selected to profile. They succeeded in getting him elected to the boards of the Cosmopolitan Chamber of Commerce, the Calumet Area Industrial Commission, Homewood Business Association and the Boys and Girls Club of Chicago. He did not like his new administrative position because in addition to the civic assignments it required a lot of traveling. As a matter of fact, they wanted him to move to New Jersey which meant replanting his roots outside of what had always been his home turf.

During the late 1980's AT&T offered an early retirement program with a bonus of one year's pay. Bonaparte saw this as an option to traveling and an opportune time to exit from employee status to that of an entrepreneur. Moreover his achievement clock was telling him that the time was ripe for him to jump into the waters of Lake Commerce. On the other hand, nobody told him that the lake was infested with capital minded barracudas.

In January 1987, The Bonaparte Connection was born in the basement of his home in Matteson, Illinois. A suburb located forty minutes south of the Chicago Loop. His first employees were his sister-in-law and brother. Illinois Bell gave the company some work but nothing major. Through the Robbie Smith, Public Relation firm, his company was brought to the attention of the Rohlm Company, a subsidiary of I.B.M., for whom he subsequently did some work.

The water and waves in Lake Commerce were rough and high until The Bonaparte Connection got a contract with the State of Illinois for a $140,000 installation. At first glance the Illinois State contract appeared to be a lifeboat, when in reality it turned out to be an albatross. The state did not pay for the work that was performed by Bonaparte's embryonic company for 140 days. The Bonaparte boat was about to sink when the Chicago Capital Fund appeared on the horizon.

Bonaparte states: *The Chicago Capital Fund Consortium came together because of the Mayor's desire to see something done for the benefit of the Black business community. The Capital people told me that they were willing to invest $350,000 in Bonaparte Connection, Inc.. That was the exact amount of money that I had calculated I would need to become shipshape and stay afloat.*

There were several conditions I had to meet before they would disburse any funds: I had to hire some people that they recommended for professional management, they also strongly suggested that I use one of the big eight accounting firms like the Arthur Andersen organization. In addition they insisted that I hire some engineers and marketing folks.

I complied and the money started rolling in like water after I had signed an agreement with Capital Fund at the office of the Sidley and Austin Law Firm. They gave me $20,000 to cover my tax problem and another $15,000 for a sundry of other debts. I was borrowing money from them frequently to meet the payroll. In exchange for the money loaned to me they acquired controlling interest in Bonaparte Connection Inc.

In December 1990, the Chicago Capital Fund forcibly took control of Bonaparte Connection Inc.. A company in which it had pumped $100,000 into between 1988 and 1989. In William Bonaparte's place they installed Brian King as

President. He is a native of Evanston, Illinois with lending experience at Chicago based Harris Trust and Savings Bank and the Chemical Bank in New York. He is a graduate of Morehouse College in Atlanta, Georgia, and the Wharton School of Finance in Philadelphia, Pennsylvania. The Bonaparte Connection Inc. was renamed Genesis Communication Inc.. Like it was predecessor it was a cable and electrical contractor. In spite of Mr. King's glowing projection for Genesis Communications Inc. in April 1991 the company went into Chapter 7 Bankruptcy and was liquidated following a dispute with the Chicago Board of Education.

The ouster of William Bonaparte from the company that he founded was like a boxing match in that he was back in the center of the ring fighting under a new corporate structure after a three minute rest between rounds. The New Bonaparte Corp.'s revenue jumped from $1.6 million to $2.6 million in 1995. In 1996 the corporate revenue soared to a dramatic $9.1 million.

William Bonaparte owns 51% of Bonaparte Corp. and George Specht, his white partner owns the other 49%.

In 1997 Bonaparte Corp. was one of the city of Chicago's largest minority-owned electrical and cabling contractors. His company was a subcontractor on the 911 Center plus the Democratic National Convention which was held at the United Center located on the near west side. He also installed a security system at the city's filtration plant and rewired State Street's new "1940s" Back to Loop lighting program. He has also constructed a new computer system to monitor the city buses.

Currently, he has a staff of 52, which is twofold the number he had in 1995. If the current proposal that he is working on matures in his favor he will double his staff to more than 100 technicians before the end of the calendar year 1997.

The voices of Dr. Martin Luther King and Al Raby must have been ringing in Bonaparte's ears when he resigned in protest from the Builders' Association of Greater Chicago (B.A.G.C.) in 1996 when they filed a suit against the city proclaiming that their affirmative action programs were discriminatory against white males.

It is the author's opinion that all fair minded individuals should stand up and be counted when their right to work is challenged.

I am sorry but we cannot give scholarships to Black people to go to a Black medical school even though they may have a 4 point grade average.

CHAPTER 9

WE WILL NOT GIVE YOU A SCHOLAR-SHIP TO A BLACK MED SCHOOL

arl Bell was born on October 28, 1947 in Chicago at Provident Hospital located on the south side of the city at 51st and Vincennes. The Bell family lived in Lawndale's 24th Ward on the southwest side at 1633 South Spaulding Avenue, an area identified as Cobra Gang territory. His father William Bell Jr. divorced his mother, Pearl Debnam Bell, when Carl was only 2 years old and his brother William Bell III was 9.

At the age of 4 Carl spent a great deal of his playtime kicking cans in the alley and throwing dirt into the potholes that punctuated Spaulding Avenue. He wondered if he would ever be able to fill those potholes up. His young fertile mind was also fascinated with the thought that those potholes might be an underground passage to China. The potholes had literally turned the asphalt street into an obstacle course for motorists.

The 24th Ward where the Bell Family resided was earlier occupied by second generation Jews, Italians and a sprinkling of Irish Catholics. The Jewish and Italian political leaders like Alderman Sidney Deutsch, Irwin Horwitz, Carmen Fratto, Arthur V. Elrod, Ed Quigley, Toni Girolami, Jacob Arvey and State Senator Bernard S. Neistein controlled the patronage in the 24th, 27th, and 28th Wards for several decades after the wards had turned almost 100% black and after the whites had fled to Lake Shore Drive, Skokie and other points north and northwest.

The only contribution that these white absentee political bosses made to the impoverished Black wards were handouts of chickens, hams or cheap bottles of wine or whiskey on election day. Missing among their gratuities were the colorful beads.

All of the non-resident precinct captains in the 24th Ward were white because Irwin "Izzy" Horwitz who bossed the ward from his Gold Coast condominium did not believe that blacks were capable of handling the job. During the 1930's, under the leadership of Jacob Arvey, the 24th Ward Jewish ghetto provided President Franklin Delano Roosevelt with the largest one-sided election returns of any ward in the 48 states.

The first Black alderman and ward committeeman of the 24th Ward was Ben Lewis, who was elected in 1958 as a figurehead and killed mafia style in his office in late February 1963. He was found with both hands handcuffed to his armchair with a partially smoked cigarette dangling from his lips. He was shot in the head three times. His murder was never solved. His killing was a warning to other Black political aspirants about the violent mind set of the bosses who kept the 24th Ward Democratic machine huffing, puffing and chugging along.

Four years before Lewis was murdered the Bell family moved from the west side to 5050 South Ellis Avenue in the Kenwood-Oakwood area on the south side near the University of Chicago. The street gang that controlled that turf was the Vendells. His brother Bill, who was seven years older than Carl was a gang leader. Nobody at the Kominski Elementary School would mess with Carl because of his big brother's reputation as a tough street corner gangbanger. At age 11 when Carl was a 6th grader, his brother Bill, who was then 18 years old, decided to join the United States Army. In his brother's absence Carl decided to put some space between himself and the street gang activities.

At age 13 Carl was enrolled at Hyde Park High School which by that time had flipped over from a 90 percent white student population to one that was predominantly black. The unwritten rule at Hyde Park High was that it was good for your health to belong to a gang. The two gangs operating within the school were the Black P-Stone Rangers and the Disciples.

Carl made the following observation: *You were recruited into a gang the same as you might be rushed into a fraternity. I joined the Black P-Stone Rangers in which Jeff Fort was a member. The gang password would sometimes change everyday. For example, if I said apple you had better say juice if you did not want your butt kicked. As a part of the initiation it was mandatory for you to have a boxing match with an older member of the gang. This for me was a cake walk because I was considered good at fisticuffs, my big brother had taught me well. My troubles with fellow gang members was minimum. I saw myself as being in the gang but not part of their antisocial activities.*

From age 13 to 17 I considered myself a floater, I had friends across a wide spectrum. I melted perfectly in both language and style with the boys at the pool hall, I was comfortable hanging out with my fellow Black P-Stone Ranger gang members. I could also blend at a party with the ease of a sheik in middle-class Chatham which we called 'The Gold Plated Ghetto'.

I classified myself as one of the 'dead end' kids until I met Mr. Milton Benz, my Hyde Park High geometry teacher, he was an excellent black role model. One day I did something stupid in his room and he embarrassed me in front of the entire class. He said:

'Mr. Bell are you going to use your brain or are you going to be a jerk for the rest of your life?' I was livid, I decided I would get even with him on his terms. From that day forward every time he neglected to cross a 't' or dot an 'i' or explain a theorem proof properly, I brought it to his attention in the classroom.

During the period that I was performing my Plato roles with Mr. Benz a veil was lifted from my eyes and I suddenly saw clearly that I had learned how to learn.

For my last two years in high school I went to class without ever giving a thought to ducking to go to the Tivoli Theater or party at somebody's house during my classroom hours which were from 8a.m. to 2p.m.. Following class I would hit the books everyday in the school library from 2 to 4. I was making straight A's in all of my subjects. From 4 to 9 in the evening, I was usually physically present on the basketball court with some of the gang members, but mentally my mind was not on the ball, it was on the books.

In January 1965, at age 17, Carl graduated from Hyde Park High School. He spent the next six months sitting on his behind doing absolutely nothing. Then suddenly on a hot July afternoon, it dawned on him that time and tide wait for no man and that he was letting all of the possibilities of escaping from poverty pass him by.

As he sat alone bracing his chin in his hands one morning, he made a revolutionary decision about his education without sharing the benefit of his thoughts with anybody. He decided that he was going to finish college with a Bachelor's Degree within a two year period. He reasoned that if he could spend eight hours a day hitting the books in high school there was no reason why he could not put in the same amount of time and energy in college.

Before he could get his educational plan off the ground, during his first summer semester at Wilson Junior College the sky fell on his head in August 1965. His brother who had become a police officer after being discharged from the army was killed by two white officers in uniform who mistook the black officer out of uniform with a gun in his hand pursuing a criminal, as the criminal. Carl was told by the mortician that his brother was shot six times in the back.

Before the last leaves of brown came tumbling down in the fall of 1965 Carl's mother died of a kidney disease at the age of 48. His natural father died as the winter snow melted in late February of 1966 with a heart attack at age 52. For the years 1965 and 1966 Carl Bell could rightfully say, *"Into each life some rain must fall, but too much has fallen in mine."*

His stepfather Marion Pratt survived both of his natural parents. However, in August 1965 at his brother's funeral when his biological father attempted to introduce him to one of his friends as his son, Carl without skipping a heart beat, corrected him by pointing to Pratt as his real dad. Pratt was always at the boy's side when he needed him. Burt Pratt, his stepfather's brother also put his arms around the 17 year old parentless kid and took him into his home to live with his family at 8159 South St. Lawrence in the Chatham area.

By June 1966, Carl had accumulated 2 years of college credit in 13 months at the Chicago City Colleges. In June 1967 he graduated in the top 5 percent of his class from the University of Illinois in Chicago with a major in Biology and minors in Math and Chemistry.

Bell applied for admission to the University of Illinois Medical School. His friend Carl Ivey, who is now a very successful pediatrician also applied at the same time. Ivey had maintained a B average and Carl had held steady with a B+ average.

When Carl was notified he would not be accepted at the U. of I. Med School he went directly to the dean and said: *"What's up?"*

The dean retorted: *"Your grade point average was not high enough."*

Carl shot back, *"I know my grade average was higher than Ivey's."*

The dean paused and stroked his chin and said: *"Wait a minute I need to check the records."* He came back and acknowledged that Bell indeed had a higher grade average than Ivey.

Bell then snapped back: *"Why didn't you let me in? It took Ivey 4 years to get out of college it only took me 2. I had a Math and Chemistry minor. Ivey only had one minor and that was Chemistry. We are both Biology majors."*

It took the dean several minutes to come up for air following that barrage of contradiction. Then he said: *"Well your MCAT score was not as high as Ivey's."*

Bell recoiled and shouted: *"You are wrong again Ivey's MCAT scores was this and my score was that."*

The dean then placidly said: *"Ivey was more active in extracurricular activities than you were, he was in the ROTC and the band. Therefore, I am suggesting that you try again next year."*

Bell screamed: *"That statement is not true! I was a lifeguard and I participated in several intramural sports. If I don't get in medical school this year I will be dead in Vietnam this time next year."*

Burt Pratt, Carl's step-uncle who served as a Colonel in the United States Army during World War II asked a friend of his on the U. of I. staff to check out the reason why Carl was rejected. Pratt's friend reported back in short order that the University of Illinois Medical School had only accepted 3 Black students per year for the past 20 years and that the U. of I. Board of Trustees had never given any thought to increasing their quota of blacks.

Carl like most pre-med students had applied at several medical schools. Although he did not know anything about the reputation of Meharry Medical School in Nashville, Tennessee (except that it was black) he also filed for admission at that institution. He was immediately accepted. All he needed was $500.00 for his first year tuition plus bus or train fare. Unfortunately he did not have a solitary five dollar bill in his pocket.

His next move was to get some money from the National Scholarship Foundation which was located near the University of Chicago at 57th and Woodlawn. Carl Bell describes that experience as follows:

"Upon entering the foundation office I was invited to sit down at the desk of a very proper speaking middle age Caucasian male who was wearing a navy blue oxford suit, white shirt, and a red stripe power tie."

He said: *"What can I do for you today young man?"*

I replied: *"I need some scholarship money to go to school."*

"What is your grade point average?" the gentleman asked.

"It is B+," Carl rebounded.

"That is pretty good," he responded.

"What did you major in?" he queried.

Carl sallied, *"I majored in Biology and minored in Math and Chemistry."*

"That is very good," he replied.

"What about your family?"

Carl softly said, *"Both of my parents are dead, I ain't got nobody, it's just me."*

The interviewer lifted his eyes from the questionnaire he was filling out and said:

"We are not going to have any problems getting some money for you. How much do you need?"

Carl said, *"$500.00."*

The interviewer smiled, and said, *"There won't be a problem getting that amount of money. As a matter of fact it is going to be easy. You are one of the best applicants we have seen in a long time."*

"Incidently, where are you going to medical school?"

Carl said: *"Meharry Medical School in Nashville."*

The interviewer gulped and said: *"I am sorry, but we can not give Black people money to go to a Black Medical School."*

Carl bristled and countered: *"You people would not let me in the University of Illinois where the tuition for Illinois resi-*

dents is only $140.00 per year. If they had accepted me at the U. of I. I would not be here begging for $500.00 to go to Meharry. What are you people doing to me? What's going on?"

Carl was determined to be a doctor so he left Chicago by bus heading for Nashville with less than $100.00 in his pocket. The Meharry Medical School people were interested enough in the teenager to give him a $500.00 scholarship which enabled him to get through his first year of medical school.

The second year must have been financially painful because Carl could not recall in detail how he afforded it. He remembers he had to work and work hard in addition to maintaining their academic standard.

The third year was easier because Robert Burnett, a friend and fellow medical student introduced him to some scholarship monies available through the (all Black) Cook County Physicians Association, as well as the Clyde Phillips', Martin Luther King Jr. Scholarship Foundation, both were located in Chicago. Even with the additional funds he still did not have enough money therefore, he had to continue working.

He handled his meager earnings frugally. In addition to his tuition, he budgeted a $1.50 per week for food. He figuratively tried to squeeze the water out of rocks so he could afford to buy a pocket paperback book once a week. He was an addict for both mystery and garbage novels. He would ration his reading to 20 pages a day because he wanted each book to last one whole week. The novels were his only source of entertainment.

Although, no one could ever accuse Carl Bell of being fat he almost pioneered the water diet. Once a week he would go to the supermarket and buy seven cans of Chef Boy-Ar-dee Ravioli at a cost of 15 cents per can. He said, *"My only hot meal for the day would be a can of ravioli. When I wanted to stretch my money even further I would buy a bottle of ketchup, put it in some boiling water and presto, I would have tomato soup."*

One day when his money was at its lowest point for edibles he found himself looking at some cans of dog food that were packaged like a digestible feast. Moreover, a can of dog food was cheaper than a can of Chef Boy Ar-Dee. He purchased one can, took it home, opened it, put it on a plate and picked up a fork and stared at the dog food for a second time and said, *"God Almighty knows that's not for me."*

In 1971 at the age of 23 Carl Bell became a physician. He decided to specialize in psychiatry because he saw a need to treat the mind with the same intensity as one doctors on other maladies below the brain.

When Dr. Bell went to the Illinois Psychiatric Institute as a resident in 1974 he already knew what he was doing and he told them that he had spent a year studying in the Meharry Department of Psychiatry. However, the resident supervisor at the institute said: *"I don't know that you know, therefore you have to show me."* At the end of the first year the supervisor wrote an evaluation on Bell which read: ***"When Dr. Bell walked into my department and told me that he already knew the material and wanted to do something else I did not believe him, but now I realize that he was right."***

Today some 24 years after Carl Bell graduated from Meharry Medical School he is ranked among the world's top practitioners in the field of psychiatry. He serves in the following capacities: President and Chief Executive Officer of the Community Mental Health Council, Professor of Clinical Psychiatry at the University of Illinois School of Medicine, and Professor of Public Health at the University of Illinois School of Public Health.

He was a cotton picker, waiter and porter before he was a judge.

CHAPTER 10

FROM PICKING COTTON TO PRACTICING LAW BEFORE U.S. SUPREME COURT

R Eugene Pincham was born on June 28, 1925 in the "Black Belt" on the south side of Chicago in an old 19th Century lean-to. The house was located in the 4700 block of South Federal Street on a parcel of land that is now a small fragment of the present site of an infamous real estate nightmare known as the Robert Taylor Public Housing Project.

Federal Street is two blocks west of State Street and is still called the "Bucket of Blood" by those old timers who live on the east side of State in Bronzeville. The Pincham shanty was like an old ship in rough water, in that it rocked, rattled and rolled whenever the Rock Island Railroad trains rumbled over the viaduct that bridged 47th Street.

When Baby Gene was only 4 months old his parents, William Hugh Pincham and Hazel Julia Foote, separated. Hazel went back to Athens in Limestone County, Alabama where her family lived with her two babies, William Jr., 15 months, and Eugene.

Hazel Pincham got a job as a domestic servant which was the only kind of employment available for young women of color, other than picking cotton or being some white man's mistress. When her two sons reached the ages of 5 and 7 she permitted them to work in the cotton fields before and after school everyday and all day on Saturday.

The Pincham boys were fortunate in that their mother enrolled them in the Trinity School which was a private educational institution founded and underwritten by the American Missionary Association. All of the teachers in the school were white missionaries imported from locations north of the Mason-Dixon line. They taught the colored students, in addition to basic education, that they were God's special people and therefore had a right to hold their heads up high and walk with an air of arrogance. R. Eugene Pincham admits, without blinking an eye, that he learned that lesson extremely well.

The American Missionary Association set up shop in Athens, Alabama in 1866 following the Civil War. Pincham's maternal grandmother attended the Trinity School during the reconstruction period following the war between the states. After the Confederate soldiers surrendered, the Yankee missionaries swarmed across the old south like bees hovering over a honeycomb and founded educational institutions like Talladega College in Talladega, Alabama in 1867, Tougaloo College in Tougaloo, Mississippi in 1869, Fisk University in Nashville, Tennessee in 1866, Dillard University in New Orleans, Louisiana in 1869 and Le Moyne College in Memphis, Tennessee in 1866.

The Trinity School where the Pincham boys attended was burned down to its foundation on 10 separate occasions over a period of 50 years by some diehard Confederate rebels. Each time the school was destroyed the missionaries retaliated by rebuilding it bigger and better. The local plantation owners were madder than rabid dogs in August at the carpetbaggers for causing them to lose the cotton picking labor of a large number of young children. The private school year was from September to June, a period that conflicted with the plantation owners' planting and cotton picking season.

When Eugene Pincham was a sophomore in high school he got a part-time job delivering groceries for a local merchant. Everything was going well for the industrious young man until the daughter of one of the store's white customers started giving him the coquettish eye treatment. Eugene was too naive to recognize that the young lady's warm hello in tandem with her rapidly blinking eyes was a come hither gesture. Her daddy had observed his daughter's strange behavior on several occasions when Pincham delivered the groceries. The family cook, Babe Horton, a friend of the Pincham family overheard the old man talking about having some harmful acts visit the boy. Mrs. Horton passed that information on to Pincham's mother who in turn made Gene quit the delivery job.

Gene's mother shared her concerns about the possibilities of her son being injured or possibly murdered with Mr. W.T. Wright the Trinity School Principal. The principal immediately put Eugene on an accelerated academic program. In September, 1941, he was in the 11th grade, in October, 1941 he was promoted to 12th and on Thursday, December 4, 1941 the principal told Pincham that he had met all the requirements for graduation and that he could pick up his diploma in June, 1942. The cocky kid thought he had skipped the 11th and 12th grades because he was smarter than the other students.

His mother's next mission after seeing him through high school was to hastily get her son out of town before he became a guest at a Ku Klux Klan neck-tie party. Mrs. Pincham's concerns for her boy were real because she vividly remembered the April 1931 trial of the nine Colored boys in Scottsboro, Alabama. The Scottsboro youngsters were jailed for allegedly raping two white women, Ruby Bates of

Huntsville and her girlfriend, Victoria Price, both of whom were hoboing on the same freight car as the black boys. The Scottsboro rape trial became a case celeb in that it attracted national attention. The initial trial lasted only 3 days. Eight of the nine boys were sentenced to death, Roy Wright, who had just reached his 13th birthday a couple of days before he was arrested was sentenced to life in prison.

On Sunday evening, December 7, 1941, when Eugene Pincham stepped off the Illinois Central's Jim Crow Coach, at Chicago's 12th Street Station, the newsboys were hawking and shouting that the Japanese had bombed Pearl Harbor and that President Roosevelt had declared war. Most Americans outside of the armed forces at that time had never heard of Pearl Harbor.

Young Pincham remained in Chicago from December 1941 until September, 1942 which were the first 207 days of World War II. During the nine month period that he lived in the Windy City he stayed at the Colored Y.M.C.A. facility located next door to St. Thomas Episcopal Church at 3801 South Wabash Avenue. He supported himself by working as a porter for 35 cents per hour at Children's Memorial Hospital.

In September, 1942, he pulled up stakes in Abraham Lincoln's city by the Lake at his mother's suggestion and journeyed by train to Memphis, Tennessee where he enrolled in LeMoyne College. Mr. W.T. Wright, Pincham's former Trinity School principal, was now the Dean of LeMoyne College.

In his first year at Le Moyne, he maintained a B+ average and also worked as a part-time waiter at the famous Peabody Hotel in Memphis, Tennessee. During his second year at the college he got into serious academic trouble by skipping his core classes and enrolling in a non-credit program known as "Party Time." Within a heart beat Mr. W.T. Wright expelled Pincham from the school.

In the late Spring of 1943 Pincham and his mother exchanged places. She came up to Memphis and enrolled in

Le Moyne College as a student at the junior level and he supported her efforts by continuing to work at the Peabody Hotel as a waiter. Upon receiving her Bachelor Degree in Education in August, 1944, Mrs. Hazel Pincham returned to Athens in Limestone County, Alabama where she became a public school teacher.

His mother's academic success jarred R. Eugene Pincham into recognizing the need for a college education. He realized that if he stayed in Memphis he would be waiting tables for the rest of his life. (During the first five decades of the twentieth century, being a waiter on a railroad train or serving tables in a 5-star hotel like the Peabody in Memphis, the Palmer House or the Sherman Hotel in Chicago were considered high class jobs in the Black community). The positions were on par with Pullman porters and postal clerks. A large percentage of college trained Colored men worked as waiters, Pullman porters, and postal clerks because there were practically no white collar jobs for Colored men other than teaching, preaching, or working for burial societies, insurance companies, commercial banks and newspaper publishing houses which were Colored owned.

In September, 1944, Eugene Pincham and a fellow waiter by the name of George Saddler, quit their jobs at the Peabody Hotel and went down to Nashville to enroll in Tennessee State. Saddler was drafted into the army a month after he enrolled at the state school. However, his presence before going into the armed service had been helpful to Pincham because Saddler had been a former student at State and was able to give Pincham some tips about life on a big campus.

Academically, Pincham had smooth sailing at Tennessee State because of the excellent training he had received at Trinity High School and Le Moyne College. He told the author that he did not have to buy a book during the entire three years that he was at State because the material that they were teaching was really a rehash of what he had studied earlier.

Pincham's grade point average at Tennessee State was high enough to enable him to get into the Northwestern University Law School in Chicago, Illinois in September, 1948. He was the only Negro in his class, as was the late States Attorney Cecil Partee, in the class before him, and the late Harold Washington, the first Black Mayor of Chicago, in the class after him. His first semester in law school was difficult because of the difference in teaching methods between undergraduate school and law school. In undergraduate school you were taught precision and accuracy, whereas in law school you learned reasoning. For example, in law school they did not address the fact that 2x2=4, they wanted to know why.

Eugene's father had remained in Chicago after separating from Gene's mother. He discouraged Gene when he initially entered law school because he reasoned that his son could not compete with those white boys who had graduated from Ivy League universities, eastern prep schools and were scions of families steeped with several generations of professionals. However, Gene's father became supportive once he became convinced that his boy would succeed.

In his second year in law school he married Alzata Cudalla Henry, his college sweetheart from Louisville, Tennessee. She was the wind under his wing throughout law school. She enabled him to study without having to suffer from hunger. Her salary as a substitute Chicago Public School teacher was ample to support both of them. During that period you almost had to kiss some politician's behind on the corner of Madison and State at high noon to get work as a substitute teacher.

When Pincham graduated from Northwestern Law School in the spring of 1951, and passed the Illinois State Bar he became affiliated with Attorney Joseph Clayton, husband of Attorney Edith Sampson a first class lady from Pittsburgh, Pennsylvania who subsequently became the first Negro

American Delegate to the United Nations.

Clayton and Pincham practiced law out of offices located at 3518 South State Street, right next door to Congressman William L. Dawson at 3520. Clayton enjoyed the reputation of being one of the best criminal lawyers in the city of Chicago.

Clayton was Pincham's mentor for three years. In 1954 Pincham founded the law firm of Evins, Pincham, Fowlkes and Cooper. They had offices later on the second floor at 12 West Garfield Blvd. and in the Travis Building at 840 E. 87th Street where Earl Strayhorn joined the firm. Pincham was a carbon copy of Clayton in professional temperament, proficiency and as a criminal trial lawyer with few peers. He carried those attributes with him to the bench when he was elected a Judge of the Circuit Court of Cook County, Illinois, on December 6, 1976.

In June 1984, Judge Pincham was elevated to Justice of the Appellate Court of Illinois. He resigned from that post on December 28, 1989 because the Illinois Judicial Cannon of Ethics prohibits a sitting judge from seeking a non-judicial elective office while serving as a justice.

The author raised questions with Justice Pincham about bias in jury selecting, specifically in the cases of William Kennedy Smith, Mike Tyson, and Rodney King. He said:

The William Kennedy Smith case was going to be just what it was. He was tried in his own community where the name of William Kennedy Smith has some significance and some influence.

Some people might say that he had exceptionally competent counseling. I am not debating that so much as I am debating whether it was necessary for him to have expert competent counsel. The so-called victim represented a segment of the community that it looked upon unfavorably. A woman out on the town, alone, at night, meeting a man for the first time in a bar and going home with him of all places at 2 or 3 o'clock in the morning. How do you think the jury is going to evaluate the two people? The jury is going to identify and relate to the Kennedy Smith side of the case. He was a medical student, at home for the holidays. Therefore, he did not represent what the jury might perceive to be a threat. Jurors could sit there and look at him and feel comfortable as jurors frequently do. The longer the case proceeds and the longer it is in the confines of the four walls of that courtroom a rapport develops between the jury and the defendant.

That rapport develops into a very good feeling when the defendant is a person that comes from a background that does not challenge or upset the jury. It makes a juror feel comfortable being in the same room with him. The bottom line of the case was the jury wanted to identify/relate to the Kennedys and I think that's easily explained.

During deliberation let's say if you were back there right now deliberating the case you would find it more difficult to come to the alleged victim's defense. The 12 people debating innocence or guilt are more inclined, for self image purposes, to advocate the cause of William Kennedy Smith as opposed to advocating the cause of a woman who had been tattooed with a scarlet letter.

I am being the devil's advocate for the woman with the tattoo, who said, "He raped me." Yes, but why would you go to his house? Why would you go out at night alone to a tavern? Why would you be out drinking? Why would you agree to go home with him? Why would you be in a car with him? Why would you be on the beach almost naked with him?

In contrast, the supporters of William Kennedy Smith would say well, this is a young man, a medical student, he's no threat to society and his uncle is Senator Ted Kennedy and his other uncles were President John F. Kennedy and Senator Robert Kennedy. But more importantly when his mother testified, very few people have debated her testimony, no boy is going to rape a woman on the ground under his mother's window. That's where the plaintiff said the incident occurred. William Kennedy Smith's not guilty verdict was accepted by the American people and indeed it should have been.

The Tyson case presented just the opposite issues. First of all, most young, Black males are seen as a threat and by and large that's been true throughout history. In addition Tyson was being tried in a foreign forum. Tyson was not at home. He had come into the community as a stranger. His identity was known but he did not live in the community. He was being tried by jurors who were alien to him. They were not his hometown people. A crime had been committed in their community and this high profile defendant was represented by a high powered silk suit wearing Eastern lawyer. So what you have here is a racial issue. His second chair counsel was, in my judgement another big mistake. A white lawyer could not raise the issue of race with the same validity as a Black lawyer. So, how could race be the issue, the woman is Black and Tyson is Black, but the judge ain't Black. If Tyson had been white that jury would not have convicted him. Had it been a white world champion and a white girl there's no question that case would not have happened. Although I was not at the trial, I understand that what the prosecutor did was take Tyson's grand jury testimony and nit-picked the contradictions between his grand jury testimony and his trial testimony. When a jury begins to hear that a defendant said something that might appear to be different at one time than at the trial they perceive him to be a liar. His credibility was tarnished and they found him guilty. In the Tyson case in addition to his not having a Black lawyer he did not have a local lawyer representing him.

His testimony was just outrageous. He said he met the lady in the afternoon hours and he was feeling on her, and pinching her buttocks. That offends people. I wouldn't want him pinching on my daughter's behind. And then when he testified that he met her and she came to his room that night and he went to the bathroom and came back out and sat on the bed and proceeded to have sex with her, the national attitude at the moment was on Magic Johnson and his HIV.

During the Tyson trial period there was a lot of apprehension and concern about unsafe sex. This man says he had oral sex with this woman. How a man could get on the witness stand and make that kind of statement in Indianapolis, where those people believe you should hold hands for at least six months before you kiss. It was just a fatal mistake. What happened in the jury room? What juror is going to sit there and advocate this man's cause? It would be embarrassing for a juror to sit there and say "Well I'm talking on behalf of Mike Tyson." How are you gonna talk on behalf of a man who met a woman at 6 o'clock and had his mouth on her vagina at 12 o'clock? The Blacks ain't gonna advocate his case because of that and certainly the whites aren't...how many Blacks did they have on the jury one or two? No one should be surprised that he was found guilty.

Sectional biases are very strong in this nation, believe me. Not only do you have sectional bias against the defendant you have sectional bias against his lawyer. The first thing he should have done was to have gone downtown in Indianapolis and talked to persons in the legal profession to find out who was the most highly respected local lawyer in the community; one that was preferably Black. The next thing that he should have done, was to give the lawyer a substantial fee in the form of a check so the lawyer would have to deposit it into his bank account. The banking community and the legal community would have heard that Joe Blow from Indianapolis, our brother from the bar here, is on this case and he's making $50,000.

The white lawyer representing Tyson could not have possibly cross examined this black woman properly without offending somebody. A black lawyer would not have had that burden; he could have called it like it is. He could raise the question of why she would be going to this man's room at 12 o'clock in the morning if she didn't go for sex. The similarities are there, yet there are some dissimilarities that outweigh the similarities. And here again you had Kennedy Smith being tried by a white jury, you've got Tyson also tried by white jurors. In my judgement had Tyson been represented by a Black lawyer he would have had more blacks on the jury. A Black lawyer would have insisted upon five or six black jurors. I don't believe he would have been convicted. The sentiment in the Black community according to the people I talked to is; the man was railroaded.

Another view of the Tyson matter that I didn't want to mention to you that ought to be mentioned, is the man is rich or has the perception of being rich. So you have three ingredients that breed hostility and biases. Sectionalism, racism, and class. All of the ingredients in our society that create biases were present in this case, as opposed to the William Kennedy Smith case. White people resented Mike Tyson a 20-year old urchin off the street who became a multi-millionaire via his boxing power.

How does Rodney King fit into the racism equation?

First of all we must not overlook and ignore the fact that there were at least a dozen policemen on the scene and the system has successfully moved those observers from the defense and prevailed upon society to accept the fact that the policemen who were there looking were not and should not be defendants. I think all of them should have been implicated and they should have been defendants. Why? Because the law is very clear that they were accomplices in the crime.

The law in California and in Illinois is clear. For example...we are walking down the street and a lady meets us, and you grab and snatch her pocketbook, and knock her down and stomp her, and I don't do anything to stop you from doing it, I just stand by and watch it and allow you to do it, I am your accomplice. The law imposes a burden on me to do what I can, at least say, "Don't do it." That's the law. For society to excuse those officers who were there and didn't participate in the beating, but were not charged for not trying to stop it, to me, is deplorable and they ought to be defendants as well as accomplices.

Everyone of the police officers should have been indicted. Twelve of the seventeen policemen walked away scott free and they shouldn't have. I thought very seriously of writing the attorney general or justice department lawyer out there or calling them and telling them this. You have twelve policemen who stood there and watched this man get unmercifully beaten and did nothing about it. On the other hand in a criminal case, if 15 of the individuals leaving a party and 12 of them stood by and saw this man getting beaten to death and did nothing, they would have been accomplices.

Another thing in discussing the Rodney King case which seems to be ignored is the fact that policemen, at the time of the rioting were at the scene of the rioting and they left and did nothing. Now if you're going to indict the rioters it seems to me that you ought to indict the policemen who were there, at the scene of the rioting and ran away. They were in the environment where a man was being beaten, they did not fulfill their responsibility as law enforcement officers.

The jury selection system in Chicago has changed dramatically in the last 46 years. When Pincham started practicing in the Criminal Court Building at 26th and California in 1951 the judge would summon all of the visible black jurors to his bench pull their cards from the court file and excuse them without putting them in the box or even questioning them. When Pincham objected to this practice, the judge simply said: *"Well, you know we are not going to use any Colored folks anyway so why waste their time."*

<u>An abbreviated resume of Justice R. Eugene Pincham:</u>
Lecturer-instructor in trial and appellate techniques and advocacy: 1970 to present:

Harvard University School of Law

Cornell University, School of Law

Notre Dame University School of Law

University of Houston, Bated College of Law

University of Colorado, Boulder, School of Law

University of Arizona, School of Law

DePaul University, School of Law, Instructor, Advance Criminal

Procedure, Trial Advocacy.

Northwestern University School of Law

University of Illinois School of Law

National College of Criminal Defense Lawyers & Public Defenders

University of Nevada, Reno, School of Law

Participant numerous seminars sponsored by various Bar Associations.

Professional and Community Service Awards:

The Northwestern University Alumni Association Award of Merit, April 26, 1975.

Tennessee State University Outstanding Alumnus Award, 1976.

The Chicago Bar Association Certificate of Appreciation June 27, 1974.

The Cook County, Illinois, Bar Association's Richard E. Westbrook Award for Outstanding Contributions to the Legal Profession, June 19, 1965.

Human Resources Development Institute's Merit Award April 12, 1985.

Beauty is in the eyes of the beholder

CHAPTER 11

RICHARD HUNT'S ARTISTRY BRIDGES ETHNICITY

Richard Hunt, a renowned international sculptor seldom speaks in bitter tones about the deprivation that was inflicted upon him because of his race. He believes that racism comes in lighter shades of blue for visual artists as compared to music makers, because musicians depend upon a different set of support systems. He sights as an example a Black composer of a symphonic work for a 50 piece orchestra. It is his opinion that the work does not exist if racism prohibits a maestro of color from conducting it before a mainstream classical audience.

Duke Ellington managed to hurdle over the artistic ramparts that derailed most serious sepia musical composers by writing, playing and presenting his own material and that of other masters in jazz and religious concerts. He also wrote music for ballets (which he called water music) and mini operas such as "Queenie Pie". Ellington was indeed a musician for all seasons. He managed to keep a group of talented instrumentalists under his wings for fifty years because of his desire to play and hear his own creations in a timely fashion. In a recent interview with Clark Terry, a former Ellington trumpet player, he recalled an occasion in 1952 when Ellington passed out a musical score at a band rehearsal only to play it one time before burying the composition in a trunk never to be heard again. Duke's objective was to breathe life into all of his compositions even if it was only for a very short period.

America is culturally richer because of Ellington's ability to create harmonic structures yet to be duplicated, but still appreciated. In contrast to Ellington, Scott Joplin the ragtime piano player and composer who wrote two operas, "Guest of Honor" in 1905 and "Treemonisha" in 1910. Neither of the works were ever heard by the classical audience for which they had been intended during his lifetime.

On March 11,1991 T.J. Anderson, a top flight classical composer and chairman of the music department at Tufts University in Medford, Massachusetts said:

The keepers of the keys for classical music are not ready to accept a Black composer outside of a jazz milieu. How else can you account for the fact that they offered George Gershwin a platform, but not Scott Joplin. They welcomed Charles Ives as a conductor of a symphony orchestra but not George Walker, William Levi Dawson or William Grant Still. Leopold Stokowski wrote in 1945: 'Still is one of our greatest American classical composers.'

Black composers are not on that list of musicians who receive commissions to write operas, symphonies and chamber music. Therefore, I personally feel that I have been blessed to have patrons like Richard Hunt who support my efforts. When I tell him I want to write a chamber concerto for two violins and orchestra, he encourages me to go forward. He then puts icing on the cake by inviting me to present my work in concert at his studio. If it were not for Richard Hunt and others like him my career would have been minimized.

Richard Hunt made the following observations to the author in his studio on March 26, 1991 following my earlier conversation with T.J. Anderson:

A black symphonic composition does not exist until it's heard, whereas a black created piece of sculpture exists the moment it is completed. People will look at it, reject it, admire it and some-times buy it.

There is not a universal or pervasive sense of knowing what constitutes a Black sculptor. Moreover, European artists all through the modern period have been influenced greatly by African sculp-ture, the German expressionist is an example. Spain's Pablo Picasso referred to the time frame in his career between 1906 to 1908 as the "Negro Period." During this period his work reflected the strong influence of West African sculpture with his strong angular, schematic drawings of figures with staring masklike faces.

While a student at Chicago Art Institute, Hunt's style was influenced by many things, particularly by a European-American view that was universal in that it looked at art and culture from a world perspective of capitalism and imperial-ism. During the 1950's there were not many well known black artistic role models in America with the stature of Jacob Lawrence and Charles White.

Hunt was a product of the Chicago Public School System. He graduated in June, 1953 from Englewood High School where he was influenced by Nelly Barr a remarkable sculpture teacher. In the graduation class directly behind Hunt at Englewood High School was "Buck" Brown who has subsequently became known internationally as a Playboy Magazine cartoonist.

Richard Hunt's reflections of the late 1950's and beyond are as follows:

It was a time when we probably wouldn't want to admit it, but Black people wanted to be like white people and were not ashamed of it. However, during the 60's Black identity, pride, and

consciousness developed into what became known as Black aware-
ness. Here was a people focusing on what was already there to be
discovered, rediscovered, and crystallized into a cannon both from
an intellectual and a consumer perspective.

My own stylistic development was formed in advance of
the black is beautiful movement, however I made some concessions
to it and at the same time, remained somewhat independent of it. As
a matter of fact I will take you into my studio now, and show you
exactly what I mean. This morning Charles Duster a Black archi-
tect from the firm of Skidmore, Owings and Merrill called to com-
mission me to do the face for the altar, the lectern and some other
things at Father Clements', newly constructed Holy Angels Church,
at the same time I was doing sculptures for Fortune 500 corpora-
tions, colleges and universities. I have developed a career as a pro-
fessional sculptor, that's what I call myself, not a Black sculptor.
Yes! I am Black, but I am a professional sculptor.

I would not do a major work without a commission, but
on my own I can afford to do enough to demonstrate my ability
without the benefit of a commission.

I don't have a lot of stories to tell about how I did not get
this or did not get that because of race. Ethnic attitudes are a part
of whites and everybody else. There were times when I may have
been considered for a commission because I thought I was better
than the guy who got it because he was white. Maybe they didn't
want to have a Black person do it, but I wouldn't take anybody to
court about it.

I cannot say with absolute certainty I didn't get this or
that because I was Black. I don't have that feeling about a lot of
things that have happened, and on the other hand it is a fact that
since some Black people don't see the Black in my work, I haven't
gotten things from them because they didn't feel my work was Black
enough. There are some wealthy Blacks who have seen the merits
of my work. I have done pieces for John H. Johnson. A piece of my
work is in the lobby of the Johnson Publishing Company at 820
South Michigan Boulevard in Chicago, Illinois. George Johnson of

Ultra Sheen Products has also purchased some of my works.

I had another patron, Hobart Taylor, Jr. a very wealthy Black lawyer and a close friend of President Lyndon Baines Johnson from Texarkana, Texas who commissioned me initially to do a piece of sculpture in honor of his father on the campus of the University of Michigan at Ann Arbor. Later they named a building after his father at Prairie View A & M College in Prairie View, Texas. He also commissioned me to sculpture a piece there. He bought an estate out in Middleburg, Virginia, and he commissioned me to do a piece of work there. He died very young with Lou Gehrig's disease. However, before he passed he asked his family to commission me to do a memorial to him at his gravesite at the churchyard cemetery in Middleburg. He was not only a patron, we were friends.

He was sort of a mentor, too. My own inclinations were somewhat like his. We talked a lot about racism. We both had had our share of it.

Richard Hunt believes there is room at the top for those individuals willing to work hard to achieve their objectives. He sees no glass ceiling for those with the innate talent to create something everybody wants. There are plenty of Black role models who have proven that fact such as George Washington Carver, Savior of Southern Agriculture, Madame C.J. Walker, the cosmetic manufacturer, Dr. Charles Drew, pioneer in Blood Plasma Research, Garrett Morgan, inventor of the inhalator, and Dr. Percy Julian, who took the soybean and extracted from it an ingredient to relieve sufferers with inflammatory arthritis.

Hunt like all of the aforementioned contributors to western civilization, started at the bottom of the barrel from which he crawled. He describes his climb as follows:

I had public school teachers in grammar and high school that were very encouraging. As a matter of fact, one of my teachers in high school said, "You really ought to try sculpture." I did. Once I started doing that, the idea of making 3 dimensional things: fig-

ures, objects, I actually had an existence in space as opposed to an illusion on a 2-dimensional surface. I found sculpturing much more exciting and gratifying than painting or playing the violin. I tended to go more in that direction. Although I continued to do some drawing and painting, but I got more and more into sculpturing. By the time I finished high school I was well prepared to accept a scholarship to go to the Art Institute.

In 1956 at the age of twenty one, Hunt received his first major award, the Mr. and Mrs. Frank Logan prize, he was also the recipient of that same honor in 1961 and 1962. The following year in his senior term at the Art Institute, he was awarded a James Nelson Raymond Foreign Travel Fellowship and, upon graduating from art school, he traveled and studied in England, France, Spain and Italy. During his travels he got an opportunity to do some bronze casting. He also worked in a foundry while in Florence, Italy.

My first job as a preteen was shining shoes and sweeping up small curls of hair in my father, Howard Hunt's, barber shop at 1149 West 63rd Street. The great thing about working in the barber shop was the opportunity to hear Black men talking about local, state and national political issues. We lived on the second floor and I had space in part of the basement where I started to make my first sculptures in the 1950's. One thing led to another, I practiced music with an orchestra at the Abraham Lincoln Center on Fridays and attended classes at the Art Institute on Saturdays. My mother Inez, was a Chicago Public librarian, she introduced me to the world of books early in my life.

After several years of crawling through the business I was able to buy a small building with enough space to do some medium size sculptures. Then later I bought the building where we are standing now at 1017 West Lill Avenue in Chicago. Basically I have worked hard and saved my money.

Well for one thing, I was relatively lucky. I think that is important. There was a saying I've heard about somebody having the luck to have talent. The other part of that equation is hard work.

In my initial marketing program I started exhibiting my work in local art fairs, galleries, and entering competitive shows like the ones I participated in at the Chicago Art Institute, I won some prizes. I had an exhibition in a gallery in New York City and another at a museum, the collectors bought a handsome quantity of my work. This was in the late 50's, and early 60's. My success was a progressive sort of thing. It was actually built step by step and brick by brick.

I have always thought that we Blacks were as good as anybody else. We can make things that they want to buy. We don't have to say, well we are buying this, you have to give us that. Basically what I am saying is that I wouldn't have this building if white people didn't buy my sculptures. I would probably still be in my father's basement if I just made sculptures just for Black people.

There has been a great failure in Black leadership. We have had a window of opportunity from the early 60's until now, that window is basically getting smaller because of world economics. On the horizon there is a rise of other minorities that are challenging us for the share of the economic pie that we thought was ours. Our Black leaders have just been saying we need more representation, we need our 40 acres and a mule; we need this and we need that and they got all Black people believing that everybody else owes us something. Basically that is what we've been doing; that's what Black leadership has been about for the past 30 something years.

Richard Hunt was not digesting the rhetoric of the Black leaders and waiting on the corner for somebody to show up with his forty acres and a mule. He was busy building a reputation of excellence in his craft that would sustain him as one of the leading sculptors of this century. In the recent past the sculptured work of Henry Moore was a must have by American institutions in general and Chicago in particular. That seat on the top is now occupied by Richard Hunt whose work graces more than forty institutions in Chicago and at least that many more in the Midlands and in the South.

The following are selected samples of Richard Hunt's works which may be seen at the following institutions:
Albright-Knox Gallery, Buffalo, New York
The Art Institute of Chicago
Cincinnati Art Museum
Cleveland Museum of Art
The Hirshhorn Museum and Sculpture Garden, Washington, D.C.
Kalamazoo Institute of Arts, Kalamazoo, MI
Los Angeles County Museum, Los Angles, CA
National Gallery, Washington, D.C.
National Museum of American Art, Washington, D.C.
National Museum of Israel, Jerusalem
Nelson-Atkins Museum of Art, Kansas City
New Jersey State Museum, Trenton
The Metropolitan Museum of Art, New York
Museum of the Twentieth Century, Vienna
Storm King Art Center, Montainville, New York
Whitney Museum of American Art, New York
The Wichita Art Museum, Wichita, Kansas
The Carter G. Woodson Regional Library, Chicago, Illinois

Selected Pieces of Public Works and Commissions by Richard Hunt:
1967-69 Play welded corten steel, John J. Madden Mental Health Center, Hines, Illinois
1971 Sea Wall metal, plaster, wood, glass, Michael Reese Hospital, Chicago, Illinois
1972 Expansive Construction welded bronze, Johnson Publishing Company, Chicago, Illinois
Dynamic Pyramid welded bronze, Johnson Products Company, Chicago, Illinois
1975 Why cast bronze, University of Chicago, Chicago, Illinois, 2nd cast
Sculpture Garden, University of California at

Los Angeles, Los Angeles, California
    Slabs of the Sunburnt West welded bronze,
Memorial to Carl Sandburg, University of Illinois at
Chicago, Chicago, Illinois
    From Here To There welded bronze, 2 parts
Martin Luther King Community Service Center,
Chicago, Illinois
    Historical Circle and Peregrine Section, welded
corten steel, 2 parts, Bentley Historical Library,
University of Michigan, Ann Arbor, Michigan
1976 Texaurus welded corten steel, The Woodlands.
Woodlands, Texas
    Richmond Cycle, welded bronze, 2 parts, Social
Security Service Center, Richmond, California
    Harlem Hybrid welded bronze, Roosevelt
Square, New York, New York
1977 Sentimental Scale and Wedge, welded bronze, 2
parts, Justice Center, Cleveland, Ohio
    Cartwright Mound welded bronze, Cartwright
Park, Evanston, Illinois
    I Have Been To The Mountain, welded corten
steel, Martin Luther King Memorial,
Memphis,Tennessee
    Jacob's Ladder welded bronze, Carter Woodson
Library, Chicago, Illinois
    Ascending Descending Form, welded bronze,
brass and copper, Caleb Community Center, Miami,
Florida
1978 Centennial welded corten steel, Prairie View A
& M University, Prairie View, Texas
    A Bridge Across and Beyond, welded bronze,
Howard University, Washington, D.C.
    Mountain Flight, welded corten steel,
Greenville County Museum, Greenville, South
Carolina
1979 Orpheus welded steel, Cultural Activities

Center, Temple, Texas

Fox Box Hybrid welded corten steel, 900 Lake Shore Drive, Chicago, Illinois

Windover welded bronze, Allen Center, Northwestern University,   Evanston, Illinois

1980 Farmers Dream welded corten steel, International Minerals Corp., Northbrook, Illnois

1981 Bridging and Branching welded stainless steel, Woodfield Lake, Schaumburg, Illinois

Spirit of Freedom welded bronze, City of Kansas, Kansas City, Missouri

Pillar welded corten steel, Michael Reese Hospital, Chicago, Illinois

1982 Giant Steps welded stainless steel, Detroit Receiving Hospital, Detroit, Michigan

Growing in Illinois welded corten steel Veterinary Medicine Building, University of Illinois, Urbana, Illinois

1983 Organic Construction welded bronze, Urban Investment and Development Company, 333 Wacker Drive, Chicago, Illinois

The Bush Was Not Consumed welded brass and bronze

Eternal Life welded bronze, Temple B'nai Israel, Kankakee, Illinois

1984 Meander welded corten steel, Lake Forest College, Lake Forest, Illinois

From the Sea welded and cast bronze

Icon welded and cast bronze, McDonald's Corporation, Oak Brook, Illinois

Senator Adelbert Roberts Memorial cast bronze, State Capitol Rotunda, Springfield, Illinois

Illinois River Landscape welded steel, State of Illinois Center, Chicago, Illinois

Sea Change welded corten steel, University of the District of Columbia, Washington, D.C.

1985 <u>Dune Growth</u> welded stainless steel
    <u>Interchange</u> welded stainless steel, Gary
Transportation Center, Gary, Indiana
1986 <u>Build-Grow</u> welded stainless steel, York College-
CUNY, New York City (Queens)
    <u>Growing Orbit</u> welded bronze, FMC
Corporation, Chicago, Illinois
    <u>Sea Change</u> welded bronze, Northern Trust,
Chicago, Illinois
1987-1988 <u>Elements</u> welded stainless steel, University
of Connecticut Storrs, Connecticut
1988-1989 <u>Eagle Columns</u> welded bronze, Jonquil
Park, Chicago, Illinois
    <u>Freedman's Column</u> welded bronze, Howard
University, Washington, D.C.
    <u>Wisdom Bridge</u> welded stainless steel, Atlanta
Public Library, Atlanta, Georgia
1990 <u>Untitled</u> welded bronze, Kalamazoo College,
Kalamazoo, Michigan

Will The Myth of The "Black Jelly Bean" Theory Prevail?

The top adjutant general graduate was Fed Ex'd to Korea whereas his white classmates selected their own posts in places like Rio de Janeiro, Paris, Madrid, Berlin and London.

CHAPTER 12

WILL THE MYTH OF THE "BLACK JELLY BEAN" THEORY PREVAIL?

Walter H. Clark was born in Athens, Georgia, June 5, 1928, the youngest son of John Quincy and Beulah Hill Clark. His parents were graduates of Wilberforce University, a traditional Black college in Wilberforce, Ohio. John Quincy, who earned a master's degree from the University of Illinois, taught, coached and subsequently became the principal of the Crispus Attucks High School for Colored people in Carbondale, Illinois, the same school that Walter and his brother John Quincy, Jr. attended. The Clark brothers worked as newspaper boys for the Chicago Defender during their pre-teenage years.

The white children in Carbondale attended Carbondale Community High School. Although the community of Carbondale had two schools and two boards of education, one for the white school and another for the Blacks, the Black school board was controlled by whites.

In 1946, during his senior year in high school, Walter was offered a football and basketball scholarship to Southern Illinois University in Carbondale. As the first Black to play on the SIU football team, he suffered many indignities. Walter could not travel with the team to play against Southeast Missouri State University in Cape Giradau because the Missouri State team refused to play against a football team with a Black player.

Interstate basketball in Illinois was just as tainted with racism as interstate football. Black high school basketball teams were not permitted to participate in the Sweet Sixteen Basketball Tournament held annually in Champaign, Illinois. Chicago's All Colored DuSable High School basketball team broke the tournament Jim Crow barrier in 1953.

The powerful stench of racism during Walter's freshman year at Southern Illinois University was so overwhelming that he was prompted to transfer to Compton Junior College in Compton, California, where he earned an Associate of Arts Degree. He spent his third year at the University of California in Los Angeles. Walter could not afford to finish his undergraduate studies on the West Coast, so he returned to SIU and received a Bachelor's Degree in Business Administration in 1951.

The white accounting students in Clark's senior class were able to secure work in small businesses in surrounding towns, but there was no work in the Carbondale area or elsewhere for a Black accounting major.

Walter offered to work without pay for, Mr. Curtis, a white friend of his father's, in order to gain some-on-the job experience. Curtis, who was also a member of the board of education, refused his request, saying that he was afraid that he would lose his client base if he had a Negro working on their books. John Clark Sr. reminded his old friend Curtis that he was the only CPA in town and therefore considered it unlikely that his clients would take the trouble to seek an accountant in another town. In spite of Clark's pleas, Curtis held to the position that having a Black on his staff would ruin his business.

The day after Walter graduated from SIU, he caught the first train smoking and went north in search of employment in Chicago. His first stop was to Howard Gould, a former Chicago Urban League industrial secretary, who was currently operating an employment placement service at 412 East 47th street. There were very few white-collar jobs above clerk/typist available for college trained Blacks in the 1950's.

Gould gave Clark a number of leads consisting of manufacturing companies and accounting firms. The CPA firms did not even extend him the courtesy of allowing him to fill out an application. A few manufacturing firms gave him a battery of tests, some of which took up to four hours to complete. The tests were given to Blacks as a charade for companies with government contracts who used the tests to mask their noncompliance with the toothless Fair Employment Practices Commission (FEPC). For Walter, the explanations for not being hired were always the same: he was over-educated for the positions that were available.

After months of searching for employment, Clark met Wilbur Slaughter, a real estate broker who introduced him to Mrs. Louise Quarles at the Illinois Federal Savings and Loan Association, a Black owned institution located in the Rosenwald Apartment Building at 62 East 47th Street. Mrs. Louise Quarles became Clark's immediate boss at Illinois Service Federal.

Robert R. Taylor, the Secretary/Treasurer of the Illinois Federal Savings and Loan Association, was the first Black to be elected to the board of the Chicago Housing Authority. He served as its chairman from 1948 to 1950. Taylor's principal occupation was that of real estate manager of the Julius Rosenwald Michigan Boulevard Apartments, a post he held from 1927 to 1957. After his death, a public housing project was named after him.

Walter Clark had worked at Illinois Federal for six

months when he was drafted into the U.S. Army. After eight weeks of basic training at Fort Riley, Kansas, he was sent to the adjutant general's school at Fort Benjamin Harrison, Indiana, where he spent eight weeks learning typing and shorthand in preparation for work in an administrative head-quarters.

It was the custom at that time for graduates of the adjutant general's classes to select the posts where they wanted to begin duty. The most popular locations were Rio de Janeiro, Paris, Berlin, Madrid and London.

Walter Clark, the only Black among the 32 members of his group, did not have a choice. He alone received a direct order to be shipped immediately to Korea. Walter recalls:

That was a 'helluva' feeling. I felt like I was walking my last fifty steps to the electric chair. White folks really know how to mistreat a Black. I was the only one in that group of 32 that had specific orders to go to a war zone. Although I had the highest test score in the group, I was the one who had to go to Korea.

When I arrived in Korea, I told my superior I had just fin-ished the adjutant general's school. The sergeant said, 'I don't give a damn what you finished.' He handed me a rifle and said, ' This is land duty over here. We don't need an adjutant general. This ain't no place to take shorthand.

I told him that I was really at a disadvantage because most of the soldiers who were in Korea had been trained for at least 16 weeks as a combat unit.

Since I had no success in getting my message through to the company officers, I wrote letters to Congressman William L. Dawson, D-Ill., and U.S. Sen. Paul H. Douglas, D-Ill. I explained to them that my life was imperiled because I had not had proper training for the infantry and I also told them how much money the government had spent to teach me office skills rather than combat tactics.

By the time I was finally transferred to an administrative position in a quartermaster's division, the shooting war was over.

The only advantage that came out of the transfer was that it gave me several opportunities to visit Japan.

In 1954, after I was discharged, I went back to work at Illinois Federal, where I had previously kept books and also acted as a teller in the morning. I solicited new accounts in the evening, and on weekends I spoke at organizations and churches to acquaint people with the services that were being offered by the association.

After I was discharged from the Army I discovered that my position as bookkeeper at Illinois Federal had been taken over by a young lady and they wanted to cut my salary. Using the directives from the Army, I explained that they couldn't cut my salary nor could they refuse to rehire me because I had been drafted and had not volunteered for Army duty.

It was clear from the day I returned to work that someone at Illinois Federal didn't like me. I started looking around for another job.

I also registered at DePaul University, Chicago, and started working on my Master's Degree. It was at the DePaul personnel placement center that I heard about an opening at First Federal Savings and Loan Association of Chicago. A lady in the placement center told me that she knew they had openings, but she also knew that they didn't have any Blacks working there. I told her I would like to try anyway.

I filed my application with First Federal and was interviewed by Morton Bodfish, the Chairman. I thought it was kind of unique for the chairman of a major institution to interview an applicant for a clerical job.

I made it a point to tell Mr. Bodfish that I was still working at Illinois Federal and asked him to keep the interview confidential.

However, the next morning, Mr. Taylor greeted me at the door of Illinois Federal and said, 'I hear you were down at First Federal.'

'Who me?'

'Yes, Morton Bodfish called to see what kind of fellow you are,' he replied. 'I'm sure if you go back down there, you will have

a job.'

I followed Mr. Taylor's advice and became the first Black to be hired by First Federal.

The time was May 1955. I was lonesome. I had no contacts there except the Chairman.

My first position at First Federal was that of an accounting clerk. The most difficult thing about it was that I had no sponsors, no one to show me the ropes or provide a support system. It was like being thrown into water loaded with barracudas. My options were to swim faster than hell or be eaten alive. I swam.

Another discouraging thing about the job was the fact that although I had a pretty good education and majored in accounting, my immediate boss had not even finished high school. I swallowed hard and made the adjustment because there really were no other white-collar jobs available in an industry that blatantly practiced racism in lending.

Racism frequently comes under the guise of friendship. The female director of personnel at First Federal was a vice president who appeared to be worried about my marital status. A week did not pass without her asking me when I was going to get married. She was overly concerned about how my courtship was going, I thought she had a genuine interest in me. I didn't have any reason to think anything else.

I had been on the job about four or five months when the company had a dance. One of the girls who worked in the personnel division danced with me.

The personnel vice president called me into her office the first thing the next morning and asked: 'Why were you dancing with that girl?'

'Well, what's the problem?' I asked her.

She said, 'I just think it's wrong for you to ask a young lady for a dance without really giving her a chance to make a selection. She probably didn't want to dance with you, but since you asked her, she didn't want to hurt your feelings. I don't really feel that it's right for you to put that kind of pressure on a young lady.'

Clark let the woman talk until she exhausted the subject. Then he said, "It just so happens that the young lady asked me to dance. I didn't ask her." The woman didn't know what to say. She simply looked flabbergasted. It was then that I realized her concern about my getting married was really a fear of my socializing with white women.

Seven months after I was hired at First Federal, I decided to drop all of my moonlighting accounting jobs and concentrate on building a good reputation with that institution. I had earned a MBA at DePaul, but in spite of my best efforts, I didn't really begin to move up the corporate ladder until after I had been aboard about eight years.

In 1963, I was promoted in the accounting department, not as its head but as a supervisor. I worked for the acting treasurer, a man who had not graduated from college. My duties included preparing information for my boss to present to the board of directors. Before every board meeting he would ask me for an analysis of certain transactions which I always supplied. Frequently he was unable to understand the information I presented to him.

One day one of the board members asked my boss who prepared the material. He said, "Walter did." A board member asked, "Who the hell is Walter?" I want to see the person who was turning out the reports. I went to the board meeting and explained the reports.

My supervisor was not happy in his role of acting treasurer. He really was not qualified and he didn't want the job. However, the guy that he reported to told him if he didn't stay on, they would offer the position to me. So he kept the job because he didn't want to report to a Black man.

I became treasurer of the association in 1967 when the acting treasurer shifted into a data processing job that he liked.

Back in those years, First Federal/American Legion Post held an annual party when new officers were installed. The year I was promoted, they had picked out one of the popular new restaurants on the near North Side. I had to make all the arrangements for the party by phone, including selecting the menu.

Shortly after arriving at the restaurant, I told the maitre'd that I would be responsible for the check. He stared at me and said, "We don't allow Negroes in here." I said, "Well, I'm the treasurer of the organization. I don't see how we're going to have dinner and install the officers unless you allow me to stay."

He said, "I'm sorry, that's the rule."

So I told the guys that we had to leave. We all filed out and went back to the office and had the installation.

In 1968, Morton Bodfish, the Chairman of the savings and loan association, became ill. The directors decided to search outside of the First Federal structure for his replacement.

The new chairman was Stanley Enlund, who came over from the Sears Bank and Trust Co. The guys I reported to were angry because they didn't get the chairmanship. They would not speak to Mr. Enlund, they wouldn't help him, they wouldn't give him any directions. I said to my wife Juanita, "This doesn't make any sense. This fellow Enlund is the chairman. He is going to be the one that will make the final evaluations on the top guys and decide how much each individual will be paid." My better judgement told me to speak to him.

The next day, I went into his office, introduced myself and described my duties at the bank. He appreciated my gesture and acknowledged it in many ways as the years passed.

Stan Enlund geared the company to move quite smoothly, in part because he approved some innovations that I made. He set a precedent by skipping over the First Federal officers and selecting a new president who was really not a banker but an educator. Grover Hansen had a MBA from the University of Chicago.

As I look back at that period, the whole savings and loan industry had been filled with people who had very little formal education. Hansen started opening things up by seeking out educated people with new ideas.

With Stan as chairman and Grover as the new president, I began to get some breaks that I earned by working my behind off to understand that business. I knew the regulations, and they came to me for all kinds of information and sought my advice, I knew then that they appreciated my judgement and my capabilities. After almost 20 years I finally felt comfortable in my niche at First Federal.

I wasn't the type of person who would go around advertising my accomplishments, and that possibly was one of my mistakes. However, you can promote yourself in various ways, I'm not talking about demonstrating to your superiors that you know what you're doing. That's selling yourself to whomever you work for, to board members or anyone else. I began to do that. Many times I shared some good ideas with my superiors and they presented them to the board. That really made me feel good, and they, in turn felt good about me. I didn't say these were Walter Clark's ideas. Joe Blow was my conduit and I let him present it to the board. It was during that period that I really began to feel that I had a sponsor at First Federal and that I had earned that sponsor because I was producing. I was made vice president and treasurer of the institution in 1969.

The officers of First Federal had the use of memberships in a number of private clubs, where they entertained clients. The coordinator of these activities was Jim Fitzmorris, who had a membership at the Mid-America Club. On one occasion, I called Fitzmorris and said that I had a broker coming in from New York and I'd like to use the membership.

Jim said, "Okay, I'll see if I can connect that up." But instead of calling Mid-America Club, he called Stan Enlund, and said: 'I don't think they allow Black people over there,' he told him. 'Walter wants to take one of his clients over there for lunch. What should I do?'

Stan called me into his office and said, 'I hear you want to take so and so over to the Mid-America Club.' I told him, "Yes. This fellow from New York has been nice to me and I think he would enjoy dining at the club."

"Can't you find some other place to take him?" Stan asked.

"I'm sure I could," I replied. "But I want to take him where it's not too loud, where there's a nice atmosphere and excellent food."

He said, "Well, Walter, they don't allow Blacks to invite people over there."

'I've been over there to affairs that we have given,' I retorted.

He said, 'Yes, you can be a guest but you cannot invite a guest.'

I said, 'That doesn't quite make sense, Stan.'

He said, 'It may not make sense, but that is their rule.'

'If that's their rule, I don't think we should have a membership there,' I told him. 'If all of our officers cannot participate because it's not Jim Fitzmorris' membership, it's really First Federal's membership, I don't think any of us should have a membership.'

'Well, don't get too hasty,' he cautioned. 'Just settle down.'

I said, 'I'm not that hyped up on going but I think it's wrong. I am at a disadvantage as an officer if I can't entertain clients there like the rest of you.'

This author recalls that in the late 1960s and early '70s, the late Arthur Rubloff, the real estate tycoon, invited me to a number of affairs that were held at the Mid-America Club. And for the longest time whenever I'd go, the white parking attendants thought I was a chauffeur even though I have never worn a cap or uniform of any kind except in the Army.

The car hops would invariably rush up to my car and ask, 'Who are you here to pick up?' To avoid giving an explanation that they possibly would not have understood, I would say, 'The boss, and he's upstairs.'

That was language that was very clear to them. They just couldn't conceptualize, even after I verbally blessed them out for their stupidity on several occasions for harboring the thought that a Black would not have any reason to pull into the guest reserved section of the garage except as somebody's chauffeur, even if it was not Miss Daisy, because Miss Daisy like Blacks couldn't be a member of that club either.

Walter Clark made the following observation:

Stan must have given some thought about the club member-ship after our conversation because in 1970 he sponsored Fred Ford, a Black vice president of Draper and Kramer Realty Company as a member in the highly prestigious Union League Club.

Twelve months later he sponsored me.

That organization required applicants to have three main sponsors and other references in addition to going through an interview process.

Stan was so nervous about the possibility that I may be turned down that he looked for me every morning and asked, 'Well, how are things going? Have they set up your interview date yet? I sure hope you make it.'

I would reassure him by saying: 'Stan, relax. The world did not begin and will not end with the Union League Club.'

I was accepted and became the second Black to hold mem-bership in the Union League Club. I really take my hat off to Stan for taking the necessary steps to get me in. Membership in that club makes a quantitative difference in how you are viewed in the corporate world.

However, even as a member, some funny things happened to me. Even now, when I go over there with a white guest, some wait-ers automatically give the guest the bill.

It was at the Union League Club over lunch that I came up with the idea that we set up a Treasury Division at First Federal to deal with Treasury bonds, notes and bills. Although I didn't report directly to the chairman, I made my proposal available to him, along with the suggestions on how to operate the new treasury divi-sion.

When I discussed my proposal with Mr. Enlund I put in my

bid to head the new department, adding that I would only need a secretary and one other person to get in operation. I told him that once I got it rolling, which I anticipated would take two years, I wanted to return to my position as supervisor of the accounting department. I didn't want to be in a specialized operation, I wanted line responsibility. The chairman approved my revolutionary idea of a savings and loan association entering the bond market.

I began trading through the Chase Manhattan Bank of New York. Thomas G. LaBrecque, who helped me set up our account, is now the president of Chase. He was excited about the opportunity and said he would be buying and selling fed funds every day. I sent him $5 million to open an account and had a transaction ready to go the first day that the regulations became viable. I had done my homework.

Clark's big move came after his twentieth anniversary with First Federal in 1973, he was appointed a member of the board of directors and also promoted to senior vice president and financial group manager. As the chief financial officer, he was responsible for managing approximately $1.3 billion in assets. He had six senior officers reporting to him in the areas of mortgage lending, the investment portfolio, data processing, income tax policy and returns, financial planning and analysis, general accounting, budgeting and loan accounting.

In 1977, when he was made executive vice president, Clark became one of the top three officers at First Federal Savings and Loan Association of Chicago. Clark states:

As the third man in line, many of Stan and Grover's important telephone calls were shifted to me in their absence. One afternoon, Arthur Rubloff, the real estate magnate called for Stan.

When the secretary told him Mr. Enlund was not in the office, Mr. Rubloff said, 'Let me talk to Grover.' 'He's not here either,' she replied.

'Who can I talk to?' Rubloff asked. 'I will give you to Mr. Clark. He's next in line,' responded the secretary. "Okay let me

talk to Clark.'

He said, 'Clark, I couldn't get Enlund and Hansen. I have a situation here we need some help on.' 'What's the trouble, Arthur?' I asked. 'You know the Evergreen Park Plaza shopping center I built out south on 95th and Western Avenue?'

'Yes.' 'My heart and soul is in there,' I said. 'We got a church out there that whites are moving out of and some Blacks want to purchase it, we can't have that.'

'We can't have what?' I inquired.

'We can't have the Blacks purchasing that church.' Rubloff retorted. 'We've got to do something. I'm trying to get a group together to put down some money so we can stop the Blacks from moving in. I don't want anything in that community that is going to affect my shopping center. You just have to face it, whites don't like Blacks and Blacks don't like whites. I ain't going to try and change all of that. I ain't got enough time to live to do all of that. We need a couple hundred thousand from you. I'm gonna put in some and I've got some other people putting up some money so we can buy that church. We'll decide later what we're going to do with it, but we cannot let those Blacks purchase that property.'

'I will deliver your message,' I told him. After a brief pause, Rubloff asked, 'What's your name again?' I said, 'Walter Clark.'

Dr. Robert C. Stepto your four degrees are not enough for your kind to practice in the Ob-Gyn department at the University of Chicago Hospital.

CHAPTER 13

STEPTO'S B.S., M.S., Ph.D., AND M.D. DEGREES WERE NOT ENOUGH FOR THE ESTABLISHMENT

Robert C. Stepto was born in Chicago, Illinois, October 6, 1920, in Provident Hospital, located at 29th and Dearborn Street. The blessed event took place 15 months after Chicago's bloody race riot in the summer of 1919. His parents were Robert Louis and Grace Elvie (Williams) Stepto. The earliest address Robert remembers is 4949 South Forrestville Avenue. The Steptos were living at the Forrestville address when his father, a postal employee, injured his hand. Little Robert tagged along with his dad when he rushed to the office of their family physician, Dr. Pedro M. Santos. The boy observed the doctor treating his father's hand, and was amazed at the wizardry of medicine. He was fascinated how the grimacing pain that had been reflected in his father's facial expression went away like magic after he was serviced by the physician.

The witnessing of a doctor at work affected the roles

that Robert selected at playtime. While the other children argued over who would be the cowboys and who would be the Indians, Bob always played the doctor who attended to the wounded on the battlefield.

Young Stepto was destined to be the first physician in his family. He never considered any other profession in spite of the many barricades that were thrown in his path.

Robert attended Wendell Phillips Elementary School at 38th and Prairie until the family moved to 6350 South Vernon, in the West Woodlawn Community. He refers to Woodlawn as the "silk stocking district" because many of its residents were professionals, school teachers and civil service workers. His new school was McCosh Elementary, where he graduated with honors in June 1934.

The district high school was Englewood where the majority of students were white. He graduated number 10 in a class of 225 at the age of 17 in 1937. Because of his academic record he was awarded a scholarship to Northwestern University.

Young Robert had no real concept of racism and isolationism until he began classes on the Evanston campus of the university where there were only 15 Black students on a campus of thousands. Among the Blacks were Clarence Hinton, Bernard Jefferson, the outstanding running back in 1937-38, and Helen V. Payne, who later became a physician.

During his first year at the university he commuted on the elevated train between the Evanston campus and his home on the South side of Chicago. During the second year he got lucky and found a job as an orderly at the Evanston Community Hospital.

The Community Hospital, founded by Dr. Isabelle Garnett and two other Black physicians, was the only hospital in the area that would accept Black patients. His wages were $3.50 a week, Dr. Garnett made arrangements for Stepto to have rent free room and board. It was an excellent proposition because there were no housing facilities on the

Northwestern University campus for Blacks.

Robert Stepto said:

'All I did was work and study, principally study. I was so satisfied with the arrangement that I decided to go to school year-round in order to protect my job and sleeping quarters.

I maintained a high grade point average in spite of the fact that I worked six hours every night, six nights a week. Even with my work and classload, I never gave a thought to not being able to meet my objective of going to medical school.

It was not until my junior year when my advisor, Mr. Bochstanler, asked, 'Why are you in pre-med?'

I said, 'Because I want to be a doctor.'

He said that as bright as I was I should have known that they would not accept Blacks at the Northwestern University Medical School. 'You can't apply here at Northwestern,' he said. 'You can't apply at the University of Illinois. So where are you going to go to school?' I told him I was going to apply wherever I could as long as I could manage to scrape up the application fees.

Mr. Bochstahler acknowledged that I had pretty good grades, but warned that my dream of going to medical school could turn into a nightmare.

As far as I was concerned, Bochstahler could have saved his breath because I knew I was going to go to medical school and become a physician.

I applied to Howard University in Washington, D.C., the University of Wisconsin in Madison, and the University of Illinois, Champaign/Urbana. I wasn't too bent on going to the University of Illinois because I suffered with asthma. I frequently had asthma attacks in Chicago but was never bothered by them in Evanston. So, I decided the best thing for me was to get out of state if I could afford it.

I had never given serious thought to the affordability of moving. Then Lady Luck and her companion, hard work, tapped me on the shoulder once again and I was offered a scholarship to Howard University Medical School beginning in the fall of 1941, provided I maintained my grade point average at Northwestern until graduation.

I was second on the waiting list at the University of Wisconsin but decided Howard would be my best bet because of the scholarship. Another factor was that my fiancee Ann Burns had relatives in Washington with whom I could live without any additional expense.

Lady Luck was with me once more; I took advantage of the U.S. Army Specialized Training Program (ASTP), which funded the tuition for men eligible to serve in the armed forces who had IQ scores of 115 or better. The program allowed me to graduate from medical school without going directly into the military service.

Ann and I were married during my junior year at medical school and that made a great difference in where I would serve my internship. My parents wanted me to come back to Chicago, although I had accepted an internship at Jersey City Medical in New Jersey. I had also been offered internships at Homer G. Phillips Hospital in St. Louis and at Provident Hospital in Chicago. I decided to come back to Chicago. Ann didn't want to leave her beautiful city by the lake, and she was the real persuader.

It appears that good things were falling in my path. Soon after I returned to Chicago, Franklin McLean at the University of Chicago developed a plan called the Provident Medical Fellowship that subsequently became the National Medical Fellowship. It was a project organized to improve opportunities for Blacks who wanted to enter special medical training. I completed my internship at Provident in 1945, and did my residency in obstetrics and gynecology in a combined program with Provident and the University of Chicago Lying-In Hospital.

After completing my residency requirements, I arranged for an interview with Dr. William Dieckman, who was the chairman of the OB-GYN department at the University of Chicago. I had not been forewarned of his racial prejudice, but I got an inkling before our chat that something was wrong after he kept me waiting in the reception area for two hours.

The first words out of his mouth when I entered his office were, 'Well, I see you have an application in and you want to come here.' That was obvious, I thought to myself. 'What particular phase of obstetrics are you interested in working in?' he asked.

I said, 'Toxaemia pregnancy.'

'We do not know a lot about the pathology of toxaemia pregnancy,' he said.

I retorted, 'My interest is in the whole pathology involved in Obstetrics and Gynecology.

'I don't know if we can do anything for you here,' he said. 'However, if you can get accepted by the graduate school at University of Chicago, I'll accept you.'

'You mean I have to go back to graduate school after having completed seven years at the undergraduate level?' I gasped.

'That's right.'

I had a friend who taught in the U. of C. Pathology Department. Dr. Robert Stewart Jason who was the second Black person to get a Ph.D. in Pathology at the University of Chicago. The first one was Julian Lewis, M.D., Ph.D., who recently died at the old age of 96.

Dr. Jason wrote a letter to the chairman of the department confirming that all my credentials were in order and I enrolled in the master's program in Pathology at the university.

I completed my course work for the master's in nine months and I went back to Dr. Dieckman because I wanted to get some clinical experience in the hospital. After I acquainted him with the fact that I was qualified for a Master's in Pathology, he said, 'That's nice, but you need additional education. All of the other residents here are doing research projects because that's the thrust of an academic institution. If you want to see patients, you need to go to the Stockyard Clinic, which is over behind the "Back of the Yards" area near 47th and Ashland.

Dr. Kieckman had recommended the Stockyard Clinic because they handled a large number of Black patients. I will have to chalk it up to naivete that it finally dawned on me that the white establishment did not want Black doctors treating white women.

I didn't appreciate his telling me I needed more courses when my laboratory work in pathology was more additional training than 50 percent of the white residents had taken. In addition, it was blatantly racist to steer me to a "for Colored only" medical situation. My hands were tied and I was at the end of the gangplank, so I spent another year in academia.

My fellowship in the Department of Pathology was renewed, so with my head high, I completed the requirements for my Master's and Ph.D. in 24 months.

The problem I had while studying at the University of Chicago was that many of the physicians there wouldn't speak to me. When I gave them a friendly hello they would act as if I were an invisible man. I would go to conferences and they would look through me or glare like I was a creature from another planet. It seems that the only white persons I had positive contact with were the cadavers I encountered in Pathology 501.

It was during those extended periods in Pathology lab that I discovered I was alone but I was not lonely. To me being lonely means that you are susceptible to depression and the negatives that go with it. But you can be alone in a group and be into yourself. Being lonely you have no interaction, no self-esteem. Being alone, you can accomplish a lot as long as you have the inner strength to deal with racism. A good example is a man in the wilderness. He is alone but he is not necessarily lonely.

After I received my Ph.D. in Pathology in 1948, the University of Chicago Hospital still would not accept me in any capacity. There was no room in their inn for me. Two doctorates were not enough for a Black man to enter those doors. I was out in the wilderness without a job.

Dr. Rachmiel Levine, a physician who was called The Father of Modern Medical Research in Endocrinology, invited me to join him in the lab at Michael Reese Hospital. 'Bob,' he said, 'Come work with me because I hear you're catching hell.'

My experience during the two years at Michael Reese

was productive. During that time, I shared an office suite with several Black doctors, internist, Nathaniel Calloway, M.D. and Ph.D., at 5751 South Indiana Avenue. Also practicing out of that office were Dr. William Cunningham, an internal medicine physician and Dr. Mack Tanner, a dentist.

I was so busy in the clouds of academia that I didn't fully realize the responsibilities of a man with a wife and a young child. One afternoon, my wife said that we could use some additional money and reminded me that people often asked if I would make house calls. I told her that I couldn't make house calls because I didn't have a bag. She got me a bag. So I started seeing patients in their homes in the evening.

I worked out an arrangement at Michael Reese Hospital whereby I could enter private practice without jeopardizing my fellowship with the U.S. Public Health Service. After I completed two years of research at Reese, I applied for a staff appointment, which was denied. The only Black doctor I knew who had a staff appointment at Reese up until that time was Dr. Henry I. Wilson. After his death around 1952, a decade passed before a Black physician received an appointment at Reese.

After I had been rejected for a staff appointment at Michael Reese Hospital, Dr. Michael Levine told me that I could stay on and work with him in the lab and make a living. I said, 'I can't make a living in the research lab. I'm qualified to earn much more than what Reese is paying me.

Dr. Mary Boysen, head of the OB-GYN department at Presbyterian-St. Luke's asked me to come on board as the director of the training program, but said that she did not want me to bring in any Black patients. They would only pay me something like $12,000 or $14,000 a year, but I said that was only four times the amount of money I received on a fellowship

*and spurned that offer. Provident Hospital offered me an
appointment as head of the OB-GYN, which I accepted.*

*Dr. Herbert Schmitz at Lewis Memorial Hospital, 30th
Street and Michigan Avenue, offered me a faculty appointment
at Loyola University and hospital privileges if I worked with
him in the cytology laboratory, where I could continue my
basic research and also see my patients. I worked with
Schmitz until about 1960. Cardinal Samuel Stritch decided to
close the hospital when Dr. Schmitz died.*

*After the demise of Lewis Memorial, I joined the Mercy
Hospital staff and encountered real pressure. The medical
people did not want a Black on the staff at that hospital. I had
been dropped from the Loyola faculty shortly after Schmitz
died, therefore, I needed a new faculty appointment in order to
keep the staff position at Mercy. The University of Illinois
filled the bill; they made me an associate professor.*

*In 1953, Nathaniel Calloway and I became founding
members of the Medical Associates, along with Drs. Robert L.
Kimbrough, William Rogers and Mack Tanner, all practicing
dentists. Dr. John Coleman and Dr. Robert Morris were radi-
ologists. Dr. Aubry Manley joined Calloway and Cunningham
in internal medicine. Dr. James Richardson was the opthamolo-
gist.*

*The Medical Associates was the first group of its kind
to be organized by Blacks in medical practice in Chicago. We
had a suite of offices in the new Lake Meadows complex at
3233 South King Drive. The Corporation had a general manager and its own pharmacist and laboratory technicians. Dr.
Calloway was the group leader and entrepreneur. He became
president of the Chicago Urban League in 1955.*

*I applied again for a staff appointment at Michael
Reese because of its proximity to the Medical Associates'*

*office facility. They rejected me again. They haven't accept-
ed me until this day in 1991, though I must admit I have not
applied lately.*

By 1962, two frontal attacks had been mounted in the
courts. Suits were filed against many of the hospitals that
would not accept Black patients and Black doctors. White
doctors had begun to siphon off Black patients to hospitals
where Black doctors were not allowed to practice, despite
their qualifications.

Racism in medicine is no different from the racial
prejudice in other facets of Black life in America. It is a virus
that visits the Black population in differing degrees of intensity every two, four, six and eight decades. It is a deliberate
effort by the white establishment to keep the Black population busy reinventing the wheel. How else can you explain
why Robert C. Stepto was told by his student advisor in 1940
that Black students were not acceptable at the Northwestern
Medical School at the very time that Theodore K. Lawless, an
internationally renowned dermatologist was serving on its
faculty. Lawless served on the Northwestern Medical faculty
from 1924 to 1941. Dr. Lawless was one of several Blacks who
had received his medical degrees from Northwestern in the
early 1900s. Dr. Lawless graduated in 1919.

Dr. Lawless was denied in-patient privileges at
Northwestern's Wesley Memorial Hospital, Chicago, but his
world-wide reputation drew white patients from many coun-
tries to seek treatment at his three-story white brick office
building at 4321 South Parkway. It has been estimated that
80 percent of his patients were white. The author has wit-
nessed patients of every hue waiting in lines that stretched a
city block to consult with the doctor who had become a leg-
end in his own time. Dr. Lawless, treated rich and poor, White
and Black, without discrimination. He charged them all a
standard fee of $5.00.

Dr. Stepto shares his views on segregation:

"The housing of Black patients in hospitals mirrored the Jim Crow patterns of our society at large. For example, at the Illinois Central Hospital, which is now Doctors Hospital of Hyde Park, Inc. at 5800 South Stony Island Avenue, where historically Black patients were kept in the basement by agreement with the Illinois Central Railroad who owned the hospital. The Negro patients' beds were approximately four small rooms removed from where we performed autopsies on cadavers. This was a terrible situation.

There were segregated wards at the General Hospital in Washington, D.C. I recall when we made rounds at St. Elizabeth Hospital, a mental institution in the District of Columbia, they had floors for Blacks and floors for whites. Lying-In Hospital at the University of Chicago had the Max Epstein area, which housed Black patients on the south side of the building. The upper floor of the hospital was reserved for white patients.

Segregation was minimal at Cook County Hospital because of its heavy patient load. Lewis Memorial, like many other hospitals, dodged the segregation problem by placing Black patients in private rooms. At the South Chicago Hospital, the Black patients were an anomaly for so long that they were simply accepted. Black and white wards existed for a long time. It was not until about 1969 or '70 that we began to see the open-bed policy practiced in Chicago hospitals.

Today you can walk through hospitals and find little discrimination in the assignment of beds. This is due to two pressures: Economic pressure from Blacks who can afford to pay for top medical service, and pressure from the courts and activists to end discrimination in health care. However, there are still some white doctors who refuse to permit their patients to share a room with a Black. Their motto is segregation yesterday, segregation today, segregation forever. I made some effort to alleviate segregation by appointing a white doctor from the Woodlawn Hospital to the Provident Hospital staff.

It's strange how I got on the staff at the Woodlawn Hospital by the back door. One of my patients was carried to the emergency room at the Woodlawn Hospital because she was bleeding profusely. The doctors there said that I was on staff, though I never had been. They called me and asked that I come over immediately to see this patient. While I was there they asked me whether I would join them. That is how I became the first Black doctor on the staff of Woodlawn hospital.

A year later, John Harrod, who had been a resident in OB-GYN at the University of Chicago when I was studying pathology there, asked me to join the staff at South Chicago Hospital. The hospital was attempting to qualify for an accredited OB-GYN program. Since I had been board certified in OB-GYN since 1952 and John Harrod was also certified, we were directly responsible for South Chicago Hospital getting accreditation. I didn't have time to do a lot of work out there. I did some surgery and a few deliveries. At least some of my white peers had opportunities to see a Black physician perform under all kinds of circumstances. In 1968, I became chairman of the Department of Obstetrics and Gynecology at the Chicago Medical School. When Chicago Medical School and Mt. Sinai merged, I was asked to become chairman at Mt. Sinai. The first day that I came on board, several white physicians decided they wanted to take their patients some place else. They moved their practices to Skokie, Highland Park and other North Shore locations. The majority of the staff supported me and I ran both programs.

Stepto's B.S., M.S., Ph.D. And M.D. Degrees Were Not Enough For The Establishment

Chicago Medical School has a significant place in medical history for Black folks in particular and Americans in general. Dr. Stepto was appointed chairman of the OB-GYN department exactly 85 years after Dr. Daniel Hale Williams graduated from that institution. Dr. Williams, one of America's greatest surgeons, pioneered open heart surgery. In 1893, he performed open heart surgery on James Cornish at Provident Hospital, where Dr. Stepto was born two decades plus three years later. Dr. Williams further distinguished himself by creating the first Negro nursing school at Freedman's Hospital in Washington, D.C., before the turn of the century. He alone was responsible for the policy adopted by Provident Hospital in 1891, which opened the hospital to all qualified physicians without regard to color. In 1898 and '99, Dr. Williams was the first Negro to hold a post at St. Luke's Hospital and Northwestern Hospital.

Dr. Stepto, like Dr. Lawless and Dr. Williams, made significant contributions in his field of medicine, Stepto's talents were in great demand. Stepto said:

I was approached by the Health and Governing Commission at the Cook County Hospital to become its chairman, and was told that I could maintain my chairmanships at Mt. Sinai and the Chicago Medical School. I thought about all the work involved in operating from three posts, but I took the position because I considered it a challenge. I found out one thing while holding three chairmanships at once: The more power you have, the more respect you get regardless of the color of your skin.

I took advantage of my position to appoint women, Black and White, to programs where they had never been appointed before. I also managed to get more Blacks in the residency program, both at County and Mt. Sinai Hospitals.

I think these were important steps toward opening many of the opportunities that we have today, although there still are not as many as there should be.

Mt. Sinai separated from the Chicago Medical School, which moved to Downey, Illinois. Chicago Medical wanted me to follow them to their new location and recruit students and residents for their program, but that was impossible. I resigned from the school and kept my chairmanships at Mt. Sinai and at Cook County.

Merger mania was in the air; The teaching faculty of Rush-Presbyterian-St. Luke's and Mt. Sinai merged. I was a full professor at Rush-Pres until 1979 and resigned from Mt. Sinai in order to accept the position as director of gynecology and gynecological surgery at the University of Chicago.

To me, that move held several implications. Financially it was a step down, but morally I felt this was something I had to do because it brought me full circle to a hospital that had refused to let me perform any clinical work. From a professional point of view, it was a positive move because it signified to colleagues in my specialty all over the country that there were competent Blacks operating at the very senior level in the field of medicine. It also was an opportunity to serve as a role model for young Black students and doctors, and to show that one can achieve in spite of manmade barriers. Whenever democracy is attained in our nation on any level it benefits all Americans.

Nigger, do you see the color of my face? Let that be a reminder that you always say "Mister" and "Yes Sir", when ever you are addressing a white man.

CHAPTER 14

HIGH I.Q. NEGRO ARMY OFFICERS NEED NOT APPLY

William Cousins was born in Swifttown, Mississippi on October 6, 1927. His parents moved to Chicago in the heart of the 1930's economic depression. Shortly after they arrived in Chicago his dad lucked into a back breaking, foul smelling, common laborer's job, working at Wilson and Company in the Fertilizing Department. In addition to Wilson Company the Stockyards included Swift and Company, Armour and Company and a number of smaller packing houses. The Stockyards were located in an area bounded by 39th Street on the north and 47th Street on the south, Halsted Street on the east and Ashland Avenue on the west. The "YARDS" generated a stink that you could smell miles away in downtown Chicago with the slightest east wind. His mother got a job in the South Shore area working on her knees as a domestic, a daily grind which she continued to do all of her life, except for three years during World

War II when she secured employment in a defense factory, because of a shortage of white male workers.

Young Cousins was the first member in his family to finish high school. At DuSable High School he was an honor student and President of the January 1944 senior class. He also was the recipient of a scholarship to the University of Illinois at Urbana where he completed his undergraduate work in June 1948. He was one of three Negroes in a graduating class of 500.

In his senior year at the U. of I. Cousins applied to Harvard, Yale, Michigan, and Columbia Law Schools. He received invitations from all four schools. He selected Harvard. When he arrived at Harvard in August 1948, he sought to affiliate with the National Guard in the Massachusetts Military District as an infantry officer. He had been an ROTC officer at the U. of I., and commissioned as a second lieutenant in the Infantry Reserve. There were no Colored infantry officers in the Massachusetts National Guard and they were not receptive to the idea of having any, therefore, Cousins remained unattached.

His suspended status with the Army began to change rapidly when the North Korean Army swarmed south across the 38th parallel on June 25, 1950. In the fall of 1950 he received orders to report to the 101st Airborne Division on January 2, 1951. He withdrew from Harvard Law School in early December 1950, and returned home to Chicago to make preparations to report for duty.

Prior to being called to active duty, he had requested that he be given a few months stay to finish law school, arguing that he was being penalized because of discriminatory practices that existed in the Massachusetts Military District. He further made the case that he was being called because he was an unattached infantry officer. Had he been attached to the Massachusetts National Guard, he would not have been called unless the entire unit was called. To his surprise the order to report to duty on January 2, 1951, was rescinded and he was permitted to finish law school, provided he present himself for service the day after he graduated.

After graduation he traveled to Fort Devens, Massachusetts where he ran into what he considered blatant racism. Although he was an infantry officer he was assigned to the Quartermasters, which is a labor intensive corps historically restricted primarily to Negro troops.

Cousins immediately became an irritant to his commanding officers in that he was constantly raising the issue about being in the Quartermasters instead of the Infantry. After several months of listening to the steady rhythm of Cousins' voice, the commander decided that the only way he could get the rat-a-tat-tat out of his ears was to ship him off to Fort Dix, New Jersey. Cousins served at the Dix Army installation for several months before receiving orders to report to Fort Benning, Georgia for additional infantry training prior to being shipped overseas.

Anticipating, that at some point while in the Army he would be shipped South, Cousins bought a car. He purchased the car primarily to avoid the Jim Crow public transportation accommodations for Negroes. His mind set was such that he did not submit easily nor readily to the impositions incurred due to racial discrimination.

One night Cousins decided to drive from Fort Benning, Georgia to Montgomery, Alabama, which is a comfortable distance, to see a friend. While driving along the dark and moonless highway, he noticed a bright red light flashing through the rearview mirror of his car.

He stopped and two sheriffs' patrolmen walked up to his car. One told him he was speeding. Cousins agreed. The other patrolman shouted: *"Nigger do you see the color of my face?"* Cousins replied: *"Yes! Sir."* Simply letting the two words roll over his tongue transmitted mental shock waves that vibrated through the full length of his intestinal track. Then he was reminded that you always say, "Mister," and "Yes! Sir," when addressing a white man, which he was instructed to repeat several times, as his heart figuratively jumped through his chest.

Having humbled this proper speaking, Harvard trained Negro, the semi-illiterate patrolman displayed a sardonic grin that poured across his sunburned, moon-shaped face like syrup on a stack of pancakes. He then barked: *"Nigger, you get in your car and drive on down that road and don't look back."*

On another occasion, a white Army officer with whom Cousins had been friendly for several months blurted out: *"Bill, where did you learn to speak like that?"* His reply should have been: *"The same place that President Franklin D. Roosevelt did."* A deeper meaning to the question was the resentment that Cousins had created because of his very proper articulation. Cousins' manner of speaking grated on this officer's last nerve and he was manifesting his discomfort because of it.

When Cousins reached Korea, he was initially assigned as leader of a 60 millimeter mortar platoon. The infantry company commander was white and right out of the bowels of Mississippi. The First Sergeant was also white and from some hick town deep in the heart of Texas. Both of them felt that a Negro's place was beneath the belly of a snake. Cousins had not been in Korea a month when he observed that both the company and battalion commanders were systematically shafting young Negro officers. The turnover of platoon leaders was fast, consequently, a Negro could become a company commander as a result of the high mortality rate on the front line. However, instead of moving Colored officers thru the organizational scale, they moved them directly into the line of fire.

Had things moved along in democratic order, within a decade there would have been a large Negro presence in the upper ranks of the officers corps. This possibility obviously was taken note of by the white military leaders. To circumvent this eventuality they shafted young Colored officers by moving them out and giving them bad reports, or assigning them to dead end or excessively dangerous assignments. Cousins was a first hand witness of the unfair treatment and complained about the systematic degrading of Negro officers. Cousins' constant complaints caused his company commander to inform him that he was being relieved as leader of the platoon. He was reassigned, pulled off the front line and sent to the island of Chejro-do, where he was given the lowly assignment of Mess Officer.

Second Lieutenant Cousins, in his disgust, wrote letters to the Department of the Army outlining his grievances and citing examples of the deliberate practice of racism toward disadvantaged young Colored officers in Korea. To his amazement he got direct communication from General Joe Stillwell Jr. who was stationed on the island of Koje-do. The general arranged for Cousins to fly from Chejro-do to Koje-do in a small plane to discuss the alleged racial conspiracy.

After hearing Cousins' story the General told him he should be promoted, and made arrangements to have Cousins transferred from the Mess Hall into a new platoon. Two months after the transfer, he was ceremoniously promoted to the rank of First Lieutenant. The company commander and the battalion commander, who had been accused of shafting Negro officers, lost their commands following an investigation that confirmed Cousins' allegations. As a graduate of the Army Command and General Staff College, he retired in 1976 from the U.S. Army Reserve Corps as Lieutenant Colonel in the Judge Advocate General's Corps. The Honorable William Cousins Jr. is currently serving as Circuit Court Judge of Cook County, Illinois.

Don't attack me because I tried to light the way

CHAPTER 15

QUALITY EDUCATION MATTERS, WITH- OUT IT YOU CAN'T GET THERE FROM HERE

Jewel Rogers Lafontant was born in Chicago, Illinois on April 28, 1922, her parents were Attorney Cornelius Francis Stradford and Aida Arabella Carter. The family lived at 4937 Washington Park Court, which was and still is a high profile street located 1/2 block east of Dr. Martin Luther King Jr. Drive (South Parkway) in Bronzeville.

Her grandfather, John Stradford was born into slavery on September 10, 1861 in Versailles, Kentucky, he relocated to Alexandria, Indiana, in 1900 after graduating from Oberlin College and Indiana University Law School at the age of 29. He established and conducted a hotel business in Alexandria and achieved considerable financial success. Natural gas was the main source of wealth in that community, and her grandfather held title to some valuable land. However, when the supply of gas was exhausted, he lost a small fortune because Alexandria became a ghost town. From there he went to Tulsa, Oklahoma, where he built another hotel which was called the Stradford Hotel.

During the Tulsa Race riots, in June 1921 the Stradford Hotel was burned to the ground along with 1,115 other Negro owned properties. Stradford fled the city in fear of his life, just three steps ahead of a Ku Klux Klan lynch mob that had shot and killed his physician friend A.C. Jackson in cold blood as he was being led to an internment center under white armed guard.

Extradition proceedings were initiated to bring John B. Stradford back to Tulsa, he was charged with killing some white folks. His son, Attorney C. Frances Stradford who was then practicing law in Chicago came to his defense and circumvented the extradition proceedings.

According to the June 21, 1921 Tulsa Tribune Henry Jacobs stated that he saw J.B. Stradford, the hotel proprietor, round up an armed group of Negro men and said: "Boys, we will send and get the Muskogee crowd in the meantime you go on up there and confront the white hoodlums when they invade our Greenwood district." According to Jewel her grandfather was considered a crazy nigger by Tulsa whites. (Historically whites have always considered militant Negroes demented because of their willingness to fight against the odds.)

In September, 1922, John B. Stradford anticipated the building boom that was taking place on Chicago's southside and bought some vacant land on the southwest corner of 36th Street and Indiana Avenue. He hired an architectural firm to draw plans for a 200 room hotel and ballroom complex. A rendering of the development appeared in the November 12, 1922 edition of the Chicago Tribune. The project never got off the drawing board because of a misunderstanding he had with Jessie Binga, President of the Binga State Bank, the first Colored-owned bank in Illinois.

Jewel Stradford said: *My father, C. Frances Stradford was a brilliant man, he finished college when he was 1`6 and got a mas-*

ter's degree and a Columbia Law School degree by the time he was 20 years old. He went from Columbia University Law School in New York City to Tulsa and joined his father and then left, after several months because he was strong willed like his father plus he couldn't stand the racial prejudice. He would brief the law and argue cases, only to have the white judge say, "I heard what you said the law is; but the law is as I see it." Episodes such as these caused him to leave Oklahoma with my mother and brother and come to Chicago.

When my father started practicing law in Chicago, the Chicago Bar and American Bar Associations did not admit Blacks, he and three other Black lawyers founded the National Bar Association. He became its president in 1932.

My father founded the National Bar Association for Black lawyers to get together, exchange ideas, and learn. He also helped found the Cook County Bar Association in the mid 1930's because Blacks were not admitted to membership in the Chicago Bar Association. Being denied association with the "For Whites Only" bar meant not having access to a good library and other facilities.

Dad was an orator and a labor lawyer. He represented the Brotherhood of Sleeping Car Porters. He and A. Phillip Randolph were very good friends. Milton Webster was the general organizer of the union. I remember A. Phillip Randolph as being handsome and quiet, whereas Webster was bombastic and powerful. Webster's daughter and I were close friends. My dad was actively involved in a movement pressing for workmen's compensation.

A. Phillip was instrumental in my father being considered for the Virgin Islands' judgeship. He wrote letters to President Franklin D. Roosevelt and the Secretary of Commerce Jesse Jones saying Stradford was a brilliant lawyer who could represent all people. He didn't get it; his good friend Judge William Hastie was chosen. My father played poker every Saturday night, and the games would go until Sunday morning. Both he and Hastie were at one of those poker parties when the word came that Hastie had been selected. He was happy for him, because they were very close.

But even in those days, the Eastern establishment enjoyed a higher status than the Midwest. Hastie was the Dean of Howard University Law School in Washington, D.C.

My father was actively in the forefront of many civil rights organizations. So much so that when I was up for appointment as U.S. Attorney, the one thing in my background the could have stood in the way of my getting the job was the fact that my father was active in the National Negro Congress. That group, along with many other Black groups, were pushing for equal employment, in the '30's and the '40's. My father became president of the Congress. There were members of the communist party in the organization trying to turn it around, like they had tried to turn the N.A.A.C.P. into a pinko organization. The National Negro Congress actually became a first cousin to the Communist party, and as late as the '50's they were trying to hold that against me.

My father was very friendly with Carl Hansberry, a dyed in the wool capitalist, he was a high profile real estate man in Chicago, and very well-to-do. Hansberry bought a two flat at 61st and Rhodes. Blacks had been restricted from living in the area between 60th and 63rd and between South Parkway (Dr. Martin Luther King Jr. Drive) and Cottage Grove. My father represented Hansberry when he bought the building. I remember his daughters Lorraine, Mamie and I were sitting in the living room of their first floor apartment, when bricks were hurled through the front window. The whites filed suit to get the Hansberrys out, my father represented the family. He brought the Supreme Liberty Life Insurance Company into the case as one of the defendants in the suit, because Supreme Liberty Life held the mortgage for the Hansberrys. My father was the lead lawyer. The lawyers from Supreme Liberty Life were Earl B. Dickerson, T.K. Gibson, Jr., Loring B. Moore and Irwin C. Mollison. Dickerson, who was the general counsel for the insurance company, was selected by the Supreme lawyers to argue the case. My father was very unhappy about it, and the Hansberrys were also displeased. My father had labored with the case for years. The Hansberrys knew my father had done most of the work

143

and wanted him to get credit.

When the decision came down, one of the daily newspapers said, 'Attorneys C. Francis Stradford, Earl B. Dickerson, T.K. Gibson, Jr., Irwin C. Mollison, acting in concert for various clients, have gained a unanimous opinion from the United States Supreme Court upsetting residential restrictive covenants barring Negroes from housing in white communities.'

The Hansberrys were the real defendants, and my father prepared the brief having argued many cases in court, I know that the person who argues the case, which is the glamorous part of the law, receives the credit. You are up there for a half hour or forty-five minutes, but the bulk of the real sweat work has been done long before the presentation is made.

The playwright Lorraine Hansberry was about four years younger than I. Her sister Mamie, and I were about the same age, and we were good friends. Lorraine was considered spoiled. She was the only one in the family born into affluence; the other three siblings could remember when they were poor. When Lorraine was born, the Hansberrys had a chauffeur, fur coats and several cars. Lorraine was very smart. She was often impatient with her two older brothers. She thought they were silly. Compared to her brothers and sister she was very quiet and a little stand-offish. I was shocked when she turned out to be a brilliant playwright. She always wanted to be a doctor. I never thought of her as a theater person or being a writer.

I graduated from Willard Elementary School which had a 100% Negro student population. I went from there to Englewood High School where 75% of the pupils were lower middle class whites. The only high school in our district that I could have attended was DuSable, and my father and mother were opposed to my enrolling at an all Colored high school. They felt that the Chicago Board of Education was trying to create a separate situation for Black children. I was enrolled for one day at Hyde Park High School, which was 98% white. The principal put me out and said I was supposed to go to DuSable High School. I managed to get in Englewood High School, because my father knew somebody. He drove me to school everyday because the school was a great distance from our home.

Englewood wasn't a bad school. I finished there in 1939, finished Oberlin in 1943, and finished law school at the University of Chicago in 1946.

Since both my grandfather and my father graduated from Oberlin College, I was destined to go to Oberlin. Growing up in Chicago, my father felt I shouldn't date or have 'company' until I was 21 years old. He didn't let me out of his sight. I thought I wanted to go to school down in Nashville, at Fisk or Howard University in Washington, D.C., but he wanted me to go to Oberlin because of the great history of the school, and it was a great school. He firmly believed that you should not go to a school just because it was a black school, you go because it was the very best. In those days, the Colored schools didn't measure up to a school like Oberlin, and not very many white schools did either.

He used to say,' you don't go to college to have fun or get married. The fact that it is all white shouldn't bother you. You are not going there to socialize anyway, you are going there to get the best education you can get.' He felt the same way about law school, I had to compete on white terms.

If we got bad grades, my parents would say, 'Never use race as an excuse.' My brother and I never did. We never described people by color. 'Get the very best education you can get,' they said. Money wasn't really a goal, but education could be useful in breaking down economic barriers. I think the biggest thing wrong with America today is racism.

At Oberlin, I became president of the Cosmopolitan Club, which was a group of people interested in international and civil affairs. I had grown up thinking you were supposed to be a leader and make things better. When I went to the University of Chicago Law School, I was one of the founders of CORE(Congress on Racial Equality). We got involved in sit-ins in the early '40's, before it was popular. There was a restaurant called Stoner's, downtown on South Wabash that didn't serve Blacks. We would get an integrated group together and go there and sit down, knowing we wouldn't be served. We would sit right at the window so the other people walking by could see us. They would sometime serve us eggshells. I remember there was a crippled white fellow with us, and they would kick him. They really abused us. Then we would turn around and file a lawsuit.

I was on the legal redress committee of the N.A.A.C.P. We filed lawsuits against the various restaurants, and we ran Stoner's out of business. I developed an attitude when I went into places where people didn't want me because of my color. I felt sorry for them because I knew we were beautiful people and we were right. They were ignorant people. We got joy out of going places where we knew they didn't want us. I remember my father said that when he went into court on the Hansberry case, the judge said from the bench, 'I wouldn't go where I wasn't wanted.' You hear Blacks saying that now. Our attitude was never that way. But if you played into their hands, and you didn't go where they did not want you, and then you were not sharing in what this country had to offer.

In 1955, I became the first Black woman to be appointed assistant U.S. Attorney for the District of Illinois. I had sense enough to know that if I had been rejected because of my father's earlier affiliations I would be damned for the rest of my career. A fellow named Ira Latimer had been a Communist. Following the McCarthy days, former Communists were confessing that they had found the light, and they were exposing other Communists. Latimer wrote the F.B.I. and told them that Jewel Stradford Rogers was a communist, which was an untruth. I had to overcome that. I did overcome it, because I could point to the convention of the N.A.A.C.P. in Atlanta where the Communists tried to take over, and get the organization to merge with them. I fought and voted against it.

In addition, I had deliberately, publicly, exposed Latimer as a fraud. I had to show all this information to the F.B.I. including minutes and affidavits. I don't remember all I had to do.

The U.S. Attorney for the District of Illinois wanted to hire me and was very helpful. My father was a union man, he was never a Communist. Being Republican helped in disproving the allegation of communism. I have always been a Republican, as were my grandfather and father.

I am not very hopeful where race is concerned. I think at the top levels there will be more interaction and more achievements. I think that will keep growing. But at the lower levels, I am almost in despair and wondering when the explosion is going to come. The attitudes between the races are worse than ever.

I serve on a number of corporate boards-Trans World Airlines, Continental Illinois Bank, Equitable Life Insurance Co., Equitable Holding Co., Bendix Corp., Food Fair, Foote, Cone and Belding Advertising, Pantry Pride, Revlon, Ariel Capital Management, Harte-Hanks Communications, and the Jewel Company, Inc. These are powerful companies, and you can do a lot of good for your people.

Each board is different, like human beings. Some are more sophisticated than others, and it takes you a little while to figure them out. The same thing applies to a judge: I used to go watch a judge for a week to study his reactions, determine what pleased and displeased him before appearing before him. A company on whose board I serve was reorganizing. They would come to the meetings and say how they were hiring people in the new community.

'Since you have hired all these people, how many Blacks did you hire?' I asked.

'You know, Mrs. Lafontant, we have a hard time. We just haven't had any Black applicants.'

'What have you done to reach the Black community?'

'We put it in the local papers.'

'Why don't you try to find out about their organizations down there? By the way, did you know there is an Urban League down there?' I said.

'No, I didn't know.'

I didn't leave it at that, I found out that the fellow who was in charge of personnel for the State of Florida was a Black man. I didn't know it. I got the information and put the company in touch with the gentleman and shortly afterward, Blacks were being hired.

There was an article in one of the New York papers recently accusing Blacks on corporate boards of being selfish and not doing anything for their brothers. They generalized and said that about all Blacks on corporate boards, but they have not done their homework. They generalize and want to say, you are not deserving, rather than trying to find out if you have done anything.

The problem I find with people who criticize you, is that sometimes they are trying to find an excuse for themselves not being where you are. I understand it. Sometimes it makes you very lonely.

Two people start out the same, but one succeeds and one doesn't. The one who doesn't has to live with himself, and he has to rationalize why he isn't where you are. We can't bring ourselves to admit that someone else is smarter than we are or someone else is more deserving than we are. I think it is human nature.

You have two different groups: people who are happy for you, that you have achieved, and others who are critical of you, they have other motivations that are not always justified.

I have had people say to my face that the only reason I was selected is because I am Black. 'You are just a token.' I have gotten so it doesn't hurt me. Not only Blacks say this to me. A white judge said it to me from the bench one day. Richard Oglivie was running for governor, and I had been selected to give a speech at the $100.00-a-plate McCormick Place dinner. I am in the middle of a hearing, and the judge said from the bench, 'Why did they select you?'

'I suppose they thought I would give a good speech,' I replied.

He said, 'No, they selected you because you are a token.'

Well, I don't know about this tokenism. People say to your face; they selected you because you are a good looking woman' or 'You are a twofer.' It means two for one, a Black and a woman, and

I laugh about it, but they are serious. I can't look into the person's mind and know why they selected me. All I can say is, 'Thank you.' It is up to me to turn tokenism into something real.

In 1960, when I was selected to give the nominating address for Richard Nixon, I don't know how my name came up. I got a call that I would give a seconding speech. I wasn't a regular delegate, I was selected as a delegate-at-large. I don't know how it happened or why. I had worked awfully hard. I got the notice either that morning or the night before I was to speak. I wrote my whole speech under a hair dryer. You would think that your material would be checked in advance, or that they would prepare a speech for you to read; none of that happened. I gave the speech like I wrote it.

When I was selected to travel with then Secretary of State Henry Cabot Lodge as his civil rights advisor, I received that call while I was at the National Bar Association meeting in California. I was called to the telephone, and they asked me, and I said yes.

A lot of times, if you go public, you kill yourself, I went through that when I was young. I enjoyed seeing my name and picture in the newspaper, and then people start shooting at you.

When I went to the Solicitor General's office in 1973, I became chairman of the federal women's programs for the whole Department of Justice. Women were really mistreated in government, as were Blacks. When I left there in 1975, I went as a representative to the International Women's Year Conference in Mexico. There was a group of Black and white women there who were using obstructionist tactics, and they were just raising sand and accusing all of us who were delegates of not being sensitive to the issues of poor people and Black people. They said we were just middle class. One vocal woman was a CORE representative.

White people are afraid of Black people in large numbers. They just fold up. When I had to get up to speak, I brought it right down front.

'You are talking about not being sensitive to Black causes,' I said. 'I am one of the founders of CORE. I dare you to say this to

149

me.' The American government gave me credit for turning things around. The woman apologized to me.

The thing that bothers me most about our Black people is that we don't support each other. Here I am standing up as a representative, I am the only Black there and they choose me to attack. I had to fight and scramble to get where I am. And the fight isn't over.

Cab Calloway the King of Hi de Ho was run out of Fort Lauderdale, Florida after a drunk white woman kissed him before a crowd of 5000 jazz lovers.

CHAPTER 16

JIM CROW RODE THE RAILS WITH THE CREATORS OF THE JAZZ FORM

In May 1930 when George Dixon was hired to play trumpet and saxophone with the nationally renown Earl Hines and his Grand Terrace Orchestra in Chicago he thought it would be glamorous to travel on the road with that star studded organization. His first trip with Hines on the TOBA (Tough On Black Artist) Circuit disillusioned him. The young people of the 1960's generation and beyond will find it difficult to envision the horrible, degrading experiences inflicted on Colored musicians and entertainers who criss-crossed the forty-eight states in wagons, trucks, automobiles, buses and trains during the first six decades of this century.

George Dixon said: *"I will never forget that morning in Greenville, North Carolina. We had been riding the bus for an unusually long time that night when we pulled into a gas station shortly after daybreak. The fellows got out of the bus to stretch.*

The filling station was equipped with old-fashioned hand pumps. Milton Fletcher, one of the band's energetic young trumpet players, walked over to the white attendant who was toting a 45 pistol on his hip and pumping gas. Milton watched the fellow pumping for a while and said, 'Let me pump that gas. I have been riding all night and I need some exercise.''

The gas station attendant said in a deep southern drawl: *'Sure but you should have been around here about an hour ago, and you would have gotten plenty of exercise.'*

'How's that?' Fletcher said.

'I killed a nigger about your size,' the redneck, replied as he continued pumping the gas.

Fletcher laughed and said: *'You have got to be kidding!'*

'Naw, I ain't,' the cracker said as he looked Fletcher dead in the eye and pointed his long, axel grease covered hand toward a spot behind the filling station.

'The dead nigger is over there in that ditch,' he uttered unemotionally.

George and several other members of the orchestra walked over to the ditch with Fletcher and sure enough, there was a dead Colored man lying in a ditch within eighteen feet of the gas station. They all hurriedly got back on the bus and it screeched off burning rubber as it headed for Jacksonville, Florida. In Jacksonville, George Dixon met a Colored gentleman who was connected with the local branch of the NAACP. He reported what he had seen in Greenville. A week later when the band returned from Miami via Jacksonville, Florida, George asked the NAACP representative if he had investigated the Greenville murder.

The man replied: *"Yes I have, but I could not find any witnesses. Therefore we chalked it up as just another lynching."*

Miami had a city ordinance that prohibited a Black orchestra from playing for white audiences. Therefore, Black bands had to play for their white Miami fans in Fort Lauderdale, which is approximately twenty three miles north of Miami.

On the other hand, in West Palm Beach the police department would not permit white bus drivers or white managers in the same vehicle with the black musicians within the city limits.

The south did not have a monopoly on racism, when George played his first gig at the Congress Hotel in downtown Chicago on South Michigan Avenue he attempted to enter the hotel through the Michigan Avenue entrance, but was turned around by the doorman who told him he had to use the freight entrance which fronted on the alley.

Teddy Wilson, the piano player with the Benny Goodman Trio, was the first black musician to use the passenger elevator at the Congress. The year was 1935 and the person responsible for removing the color barrier temporarily was John Hammond, Benny Goodman's brother-in-law and also a scion of Cornelius Vanderbilt, the shipping and railroad magnate. Hammond insisted that the hotel management let Wilson use the front door and passenger elevator as long as he was a member of the Benny Goodman Trio.

In the spring of 1936, the Earl Hines Orchestra was booked to play a dance in Corbin, Kentucky a small coal-mining town. When the band bus pulled up in front of the dance hall, there were people by the hundreds pouring into the jitterbugging facility. The booking office in New York City had told Hines to collect their money in front from that particular dance promoter. Therefore, when Hines got off the bus he went directly to the promoter, Will Saunders, who was standing by the box office watching both the cashier and ticket taker. Earl Hines told him that his booking agent, Harry Squire, had instructed him to collect the band's money up front.

Saunders said, *"You will get your money."*

"We'll check everything out with you during the first intermission. Can't you see I am busy and I can not do it now."

Hines told the band's valet to start loading the instruments back on the bus. Earl "Fatha" Hines then made an

announcement over the loudspeaker indicating there would
be no dance that night. The people started raising hell. The
band members hurriedly climbed back on the bus. They had
traveled roughly about ten creeping miles through those haz-
ardous winding roads in the Kentucky mountains when two
dark green patrol cars with yellow flashing lights flagged
them down. Several red-faced Kentucky troopers jumped out
of their cars with guns drawn, and walked over to the bus
and said,

"You have got to turn this bus around."

Earl Hines said: *"Officer what do you mean?"*

"I mean you are going to play that dance tonight," the
trooper roared.

Earl got up out of his seat which was directly behind
the driver and said, *"No, sir. We have been instructed to get our
money up front and the promoter didn't have it."*

The trooper grabbed Hines by the collar with his left
hand and said, *"Listen, those niggers back there have been
preparing for this dance for four months. Now you niggers are
going to turn this bus around and go back and play for them."*

The band returned to the dance hall and played the
dance. The promoter paid them as he had promised during
the first intermission.

Back in Chicago during the late 1930's Hines had a
band singer whose name was Arthur Lee Simpkins.
Everybody affectionately called him "Georgia Boy". He had a
beautiful tenor voice and could sing in eight languages. The
Jewish night lifers loved him because he could sing in
Yiddish.

One night , during the floor show at the Grand Terrace,
"Georgia Boy" was singing "Blue Skies" and dressed to the
nines in his white bow tie and tails when a middle aged white
man walked on stage and said,

*"Arthur, what are you doing up here with that suit on?
Come on, you are going back to Georgia with me."*

Arthur tried to shush the man off, because he was

right in the middle of the floor show. The Grand Terrace bouncers tried to pull the man off the stage but he would not let go of Arthur Lee's arm. One of the bouncers hit the southern gentleman on the head with a blackjack and started dragging him across the stage. Arthur Lee started wailing and begging,

"Don't hurt him! Don't hurt him! That's Mr. Finnessey from Augusta, Georgia. My folks still live down there. Don't hurt him, please don't hurt Mr. Finnessey!"

Dixon later learned that Arthur Lee had worked as a porter in the Augusta National Bank and that Mr. Finnessey had been his boss. Finnessey had heard Arthur singing on the national broadcasting wire hookup from the Grand Terrace and decided then and there to go up to Chicago and get his boy, Arthur Lee, and take him back to Georgia where he belonged. Mr. Finnessey left Chicago just like he had come, alone.

On another occasion some of Earl Hines' sidemen including Rudy Taylor, drummer, alto player Leroy Harris and Pee-Wee Jackson, a star trumpet player, who subsequently left Hines to join the Jimmy Lunceford Orchestra, were walking down the street in El Dorado, Arkansas, looking for a movie theater that would admit Colored patrons. A white policeman walked up to Rudy and without saying a mumbling word slapped him on the left side of his face so hard that Rudy fell to the pavement like a rock.

The policeman said,

"If the rest of you niggers don't want the same thing then you better get your black asses over to the darkie section of town!"

In the fall of 1940 George Dixon went down to the University of Illinois in Urbana-Champaign, Illinois, to see the "Illini" homecoming football game with Herbert and Harry Mills of the famous Mills Brothers Quartet. When they reached Champaign-Urbana, which were Jim Crow towns, they decided to eat in the train station because the word was out that that was the only place blacks could eat except in a greasy spoon eatery on the Colored side of the tracks. After the three men sat down at the lunch counter, the counter-man told them to move over to the other side of the cafe. George asked him what was wrong with the side where they were sitting. The waiter pointed to a sign on the wall that read: "Railroad Employees Only." That was one of the many Illinois codes in the "Land of Lincoln" for "Whites Only."

When Louis Armstrong's Orchestra was engaged to perform at the "For Whites Only" Suburban Gardens in New Orleans, his home town, he wondered how he would be introduced on their nightly broadcast. He assumed that there would be a white announcer speaking to an all-white audience because that was the custom in the south and many places in the north.

Members of Armstrong's band were bubbling with excitement behind the stage curtain, anticipating their first opportunity to play over the southern air waves. Patrons in the crowded club were chatting and laughing in the spirit of celebration while waiting to see and hear their native son sing and blow his horn.

The tuxedo draped radio announcer leisurely walked to the center of the stage with his script in hand and gave his customary welcome to the Suburban Gardens audience. Then suddenly something happened. His skin turned crimson red, he dropped his script, his hands were shaking like a drug addict in need of a fix. The master of ceremony then momentarily steadied himself and blurted out over the air-waves, *"I just haven't got the heart to introduce this nigger on the radio."* He then stormed off the stage. The audience collectively gasped in bewilderment.

Pandemonium momentarily reigned throughout the club, but Louis was cool. Louis made a bold decision with lightning speed. He told Johnny Collins, his manager, he would introduce himself. Louis, then asked the band to strike a chord and he stepped out to the mike from behind the red velvet curtain. The very sight of this grinning Colored man brought every person in the room to their feet. What he said was not audible because of the thunderous ovation. Louis bowed his head in gratitude before the joyful and receptive audience. He then waved his arm in a down stroke and the orchestra commenced to play "Sleepy Time Down South," his signature song. From that point on Armstrong would always say: *"The show is on Daddy."*

Louis left New Orleans downhearted and blue after being denied an opportunity to play without compensation at a scheduled dance for several thousand Colored fans, summoned by hand flyers, to a U.S. Army base where they were to listen and trip the light fantastic to the music of their hero. The gates of the military camp were locked and the hop was cancelled for reasons only known by the great white fathers.

Armstrong left town the following morning to play gigs in Houston and several other cities and towns in Texas. However, Louis decided the night the dance was cancelled that he would put a great deal of space between himself and New Orleans because racism was both woven and dyed into the moral fabric of the Crescent City.

When Louis completed his Texas tour the musical entourage headed north to Memphis where Jim Crow jumped into his path again because the orchestra's Colored straw boss, Reuben "Big Mike" McKendrick was sitting next to Mary Collins, a lily-white woman, on the front seat of the tour bus. The bus was loaded with members of the Armstrong band and their instruments. The fact that the woman was his manager's wife and was in charge of transportation for the Armstrong Orchestra was not sufficient reason to keep the Memphis police from putting everybody on the bus in jail except the white woman.

Duke Ellington absolutely refused to make road trips by bus through Dixie, the land of cotton, tobacco, riverboats and plantations. Duke was very sensitive about the inhumane conditions under which Negroes were forced to live and travel, irrespective of their social or economic status.

Irving Mills, Ellington's manager was prepared to counter Duke's objections about the South with a princely proposition that enticed Ellington to play a chain of vaudeville houses owned by the Interstate Circuit located in Texas. The perks that Mills offered the Ellington men included a handsome increase in salary, plus a promise that in early 1934 he would charter a home on wheels for Duke and his band. The home on rails would include two luxury Pullman sleeping cars plus a 70-foot baggage car for their instruments, sound and lighting equipment as well as space for individual members to store their H & M trunks in which they would keep their uniforms, street clothes and other items. They would also have their own private dining car.

The Ellington Orchestra's Southern tour on the Interstate Circuit began in Dallas on September 3, 1933, a hot and humid day. The band played four shows a day for seven consecutive days in the air-conditioned Majestic Theater. They also played two dances that week, on Monday night they played for whites and on Thursday night for Negroes.

The Ellingtonians traveled across Texas and Oklahoma, then east to New Orleans, Birmingham, Atlanta and Memphis. Jim Crow hovered over the orchestra during the entire Dixie tour in spite of their own private traveling arrangements. In the theater the Negro patrons', permanent seats were located in the "peanut gallery," which could only be reached by climbing fire escapes on the outside of the building. The police, like an army of occupation, were always present to see that the Negroes did not violate the system.

Following the deep south tour, the Ellington band traveled up to St. Louis to play the Fox Theater. As the train pulled into Union Station, Duke's two white employees, Jack Boyd, the road manager, and Juan Tizol, the white Puerto Rican trombone player, immediately got a taxi and went to one of the town's first class hotels.

Duke and the other members of the band had to wait an hour and a half or more to get a taxi. White taxi drivers did not readily accept Negroes as passengers, unless it was a very slow day.

Ellington said: *The next day when we went out to lunch, after our first performance, we could not find a restaurant near the Fox Theater that would serve us. We did not have time to go over to the "Greasy Spoon" in the "Black Belt" and get back before we were due on stage for the next show.*

When we returned to the theater I arranged for a white man to go out and buy sandwiches at the corner drugstore.

When the proprietor of the store found out that the sandwiches were for a Negro band, he refused to fill the order.

The manager of the Fox Theater was called and he arranged for food to be sent in. After finishing the meal, Boyd, my white road manager, went across the street to a saloon overlooking the stage door of the theater. A white woman sitting next to him at the bar saw one of the men in the Ellington Orchestra band come out of the stage door and get into a taxi. She turned to Boyd and said: "Did you see that?"

"See what?" Boyd said.

"See that Nigra get in that cab?"

"Well, he is a pretty nice fellow. He's a member of the Ellington Band. Some people think he is a great artist," Boyd retorted.

"A very great artist?" she mumbled. *"Well, I don't know what you think, but I always say that the worst white man is better than the best Nigra."*

Cab Calloway, and his orchestra were the primary substitute for the Ellington Orchestra at New York's Cotton Club when they went on tour. Calloway made the following observations: *Those road trips were only for the young and pure in heart. We moved around the country from town to town by bus over bumpy roads, and usually in the dead of the night, looking for some place to sleep until we opened our gig. In those days, we weren't allowed to stay in any of the downtown hotels*

*in the cities and towns in which we played, so everywhere we
went, we had a list of Negro families that would rent us rooms.
If we had a theater engagement and were going to be in town
for a week, sometimes we would have to spread out all over
town with these beautiful Black folks who would let us have
lodging and feed us delicious soul food for as little as ten dollars a week. I can still taste those greens and black-eyed peas.
They were some of the best-cooked meals I ever tasted in my
life. Traveling on the road for Black musicians and entertainers would have been impossible if it hadn't been for the gra-
ciousness and hospitality of those lovely people who opened
their homes to us and made us feel comfortable. I have always
appreciated the kind of treatment that Black people gave
Black musicians and entertainers who were on the road.
Thousands of families in the Midwest and South opened their
homes to thousands of musicians, singers, dancers, and come-
dians. They made it possible for us to entertain America. We
couldn't have done those road shows if it hadn't been for such
warm, loving, gentle folk who treated us like family whenever
we were in town. That practice existed up until the early
1960s when a few of the lily-white hotels began to admit
Negroes.*

*I remember the first time we played a hotel in Las
Vegas during World War II. There were only three hotels there
at the time, and we were playing at the Last Frontier Hotel.
They wouldn't permit us to enter the front door, so we had to
come in the back through the kitchen. When we got off the
bandstand and finished for the night, we had to go back
through the kitchen and to the Colored section of town which
was on the other side of the railroad tracks. I remember once
in 1948 or '49, when we were playing the Sahara Hotel, there
was a motor home with a sign on it that read: "Colored*

Entertainers Only" in back of the Sahara where we had to eat, drink and spend our time during intermission after we had played our set. Again we would have to go through the kitchen and behind the bar, because I was doing lounge work with a smaller band at the time. The big band era had ended.

A funny thing happened to us as a result of Jim Crow practices during that stay in Las Vegas. I remember vividly the motor home that we used as a dressing room, dining room and any other function you could think of. We weren't permitted to order any food at the hotel. So if we wanted to eat between shows, we had to travel all the way back across town to the Colored section to get carry outs. There was a soul brother who worked at the Sahara who pushed the food cart by our motor home each evening enroute to the dining room and the lounge. Every night, he would stop and load us up with chops, steaks, salads and some of the finest side dishes you ever wanted to eat. The brother gave it to us for nothing, simply because he resented the fact that the white folks would not let us eat in the hotel where we worked.

On another occasion, we were playing a dance down in Fort Lauderdale, Florida. In the south, we played a white dance one night and a Colored dance the next night. If we played white and Colored on the same night, they would put a rope down the middle of the warehouse. They used to have dances in tobacco warehouses at that time. And there would be as many as 5000 people out on the warehouse floor. Blacks on one side of the floor and whites on the other side, divided by a rope. On this particular occasion in Ft. Lauderdale, there was a white girl in the audience who must have been juiced or something, but she wanted to get to me. Now remember, in addition to the rope being down the center of the warehouse, they also roped off the band because the band was

Colored and had to be quarantined too.

Somehow this gal got up on the bandstand. I don't know how in the hell she got up there, but she walked right up to me and kissed me in front of 5000 people. You've never heard such angry screaming and moaning from the audience, both Blacks and whites. Well, man, I nearly died! I said, "Lord, have mercy." I knew that was the end for me. Those crackers were not going to let me out of there alive. Luck was on my side because there was a trap door on the stage that led to the alley. The manager rushed us through that underground passageway below the trap door and we made it back to the bus for a fast exit out of town. Hey, the man up there let me escape from those mothers in Ft. Lauderdale because he knew I had a lot of Hi-de-Hoing to do. I have been both the King of Hi-de-Ho and Sporting Life.

Baldwin Tavares, Nat King Cole's valet and traveling companion for many years said: *In 1950 when Nat played the Thunderbird Hotel in Las Vegas, he had a congo player at the time Jack Coustanza, an Italian boy from Chicago. He was working for Nat, but since he was white he could get a room in the Thunderbird and, Nat and the rest of us couldn't. We had to stay at Mr. Shaw's on the west side of town, known as Darkie City. On top of that, although our name was on the marquee, we had to enter the hotel through the side door and stay in our dressing room until we went on stage, and our food was brought up and served buffet style every night. We refused to eat it. We did the show, returned to the dressing rooms to change our clothes and then left, because there was nothing they could do for us. When Nat finished the engagement, he told Collis, his road manager, 'I don't want to play this town anymore until I can walk through the front door.' Collis agreed.*

We did not go back to Vegas until 1953, when we played a place called the El Rancho. It was managed by Jack Entrotter, former head man of the Copacabana in New York. He had an unwritten rule that all facilities must be open to all entertainers who worked in the hotel. Nat was given a large cabin and I also had a cabin. They told Nat he could use all facilities and they meant it. Nat was the first to break the color barrier for black entertainers in Las Vegas and for Colored people in general there. Shortly afterward the Sands Hotel brought in Lena Horne and they opened the entire place up to her. She could have guests and do whatever she pleased.

We had a strange experience at the Sahara Hotel. Bill Miller, the former manager of New York's Copacabana, called Nat and invited our group over to see the show at the Sahara, we were treated royally. We had good food and drinks, and everything was beautiful. The next night we decided to go back on our own and see the show. When we got to the Sahara, the security man stopped us at the door. Nat got on the telephone and called Miller who said he was sorry but his hands were tied and he couldn't do a thing about it. We were guests one night and turned away from the door the next. Strange things happen in America.

Why don't you Colored people organize your own country club and leave us alone.

CHAPTER 17

THE TERM "BLACK BITCH" IS REPRE-HENSIBLE

L inda C. Chatman, is a native Chicagoan and the proud possessor of an engraved Doctor of Juris Prudence Degree from the University of Chicago Law School. At the time I interviewed her on November 2, 1992 she had recently been questioned about her reactions to being referred to as a "Black Bitch" during an employment interview at the Chicago office of the International Law Firm of Baker and McKenzie.

She describes that particular interview as follows:

I was ushered into this canyon sized office and escorted down a long corridor from room to room where I was introduced and engaged in brief conversations with different partners and associates of the firm. The final interview was with an Attorney O'Caine one of the senior partners and a "rainmaker" for the firm. He initially asked me the usual stock questions based on the information he had gleaned from my resume. He noted in my resume that I was a golfer. The idea of my being a Black female golfer ignited a series of unusual questions. The first question out of his mouth was: 'Why don't Black people have their own country club?' I simply sat there and looked at him because I don't think he really expected an answer. He then rambled through my curriculum vita for another several seconds and raised his head to make eye contact and blurted: 'Jews have their own country club.' Then as an afterthought he mumbled: 'I guess there aren't too many golfers in the ghetto.'

(From 1925 until 1946 most of Chicago's elite Colored golfers belonged to a Negro owned country club called Sunset Hills, it was located next to the Kankakee River near Kankakee, Illinois, which is southwest of Chicago.)

Since I was not figuratively bleeding at this point Mr. O'Caine decided to plunge his verbal knife deeper into my psyche with the following question: 'How would you feel if a judge or another attorney called you a "Black Bitch?"' Since I did not gasp or blink following his crude remark he decided to make negative comments about my hair and dress.

(On the occasion of my one interview with Attorney Chatman she was the epitome of a Vogue Magazine model with an ankle length black mink coat dramatically draped on her 5'10" frame.)

Mr. O'Caine never discussed any substantive issues about my qualifications for the job. I sat there in his office for minutes that seemed like hours in a state of disbelief. What was happening to me was incredulous. When his questioning appeared to be winding down I stood up and thanked him for his time and walked out.

I shared my Baker & McKenzie experience with several of my classmates. Their thoughts on how I should handle the matter varied. Some of them suggested that I should not do anything because it would ruin my whole career in that I would be labeled a trouble maker. Others told me if I went public with allegations on a firm as large as Baker and McKenzie I would be blackballed for life. On the other hand a number of people sincerely believed that

I should lay down and play dead. However, an overwhelming majority thought I should do something about the indignities that had been dumped on me.

My parents taught me early in life to always use my best judgment when confronted with a distasteful situation. Therefore, I felt obligated to write a letter detailing my experience to Dean Stone at the University of Chicago Law School and copying it to the managing partner of Baker and McKenzie.

I would have lost respect for myself if I had not taken a stand. As a result of my letter the Baker and McKenzie law firm was suspended from recruiting students at the University of Chicago Law School for one year. I have been told the working environment at that firm for non-whites has improved dramatically. The reputation of the firm was tarnished when the contents of my letter was leaked to the Chicago Sun-Times by a person or persons unknown to me.

Since the Baker and McKenzie experience Attorney Linda Chatman has worked with several downtown law firms. Today she is totally independent with a private law practice of her own on LaSalle Street in downtown Chicago. Her advice to young men and women graduating from the Universities today is to choose their first working environment carefully. When you are being interviewed, you should use that time to interview the potential employer to determine if there is something in the job offer that you would not be able to handle or might find uncomfortable. Money is seductive but it should not be the primary factor in determining the road you select to travel.

Note: The author spoke with Attorney Chatman in October 1997 and learned she had been appointed general counsel for a major manufacturing company.

Boys! We don't serve Negro people here. Sorry! mam, but we don't eat them either.

CHAPTER 18

SOME WHITES MADE ME FEEL LIKE A FIVE POUND SACK OF FECES

Buck Brown the international renowned cartoonist has created popular art pieces for Playboy Magazine for over thirty six years. He was born during the heart of the Great Depression on a farm outside of Morrison, Tennessee in 1936. He was the third child of Michael "Fate" and Doris Brown. His mother ran off to Chicago with another man in 1938 and left her husband "Fate" who was a $55.00 a month W.P.A. (Work Progress Administrator) laborer and the children behind. "Buck" was a two year old toddler at the time.

His eldest brother Irving, and his two step-brothers, Howard and Wayman were instructed by their father to carry "Baby" Brown along with them to school. The classes that they attended were in a tinderbox that was also used as a church on Sunday and a prayer meeting hall several nights a week.

Buck Brown recalls: *"One day I was on the floor sitting in the corner of the school room playing with blocks when my attention was captivated by a larger boy drawing a truck on the blackboard. That was my introduction to the world of graphics. To me, that boy was not just drawing, he was making or manufacturing a truck right before my very eyes. I could not wait until I got an opportunity to draw. Drawing ultimately became my way of entertaining myself."*

"Buck's" mother and her new husband returned to Tennessee in the Spring of 1941 and literally kidnapped her two sons while her ex-husband was at work. They drove the boys back to Chicago in a 1932 bulk sized green Buick with side mount tires. Irving, the older boy started crying when he realized he was being taken away from his father, whereas Buck was as happy as a baby with Christmas toys because he was wearing a spanking brand new Sunday suit and his two pants pockets were stuffed with an assortment of candies.

In September 1941, "Buck's" mother enrolled him in kindergarten at the Austin O. Sexton Elementary School located in the Washington Park Subdivision at 6020 South Langley Avenue. Joe "Everyday I Get Blues" Williams, the famous ballad and blues singer with the Count Basie Orchestra had also attended the same school a decade and a half earlier.

Following the Japanese bombing of Pearl Harbor, President Franklin Delano Roosevelt declared war against both Japan and Germany. During the war, it became faddish for school children to scribble and doodle pictures of soldiers, sailors and rifles. For most of the children in his third grade class, sketching and tracing pictures was just a passing fancy. Whereas Buck Brown continued working with a pencil for the rest of his life because he loved to draw.

During a 1997 flashback Buck Brown recalls the following: *"In 1943 when American military men were fighting both the Germans and the Japanese my third grade teacher started a drawing program. She would tape a sheet of that brown, dried, oatmeal looking drawing paper on the back blackboard and invite volunteers to go to the board and draw a picture about World War II with crayons. Since Blacks had a big presence in the War, I drew a brown soldier, in a brown uniform, standing in front of a brown tent, on brown dirt. I wound up with an almost solid brown picture. The teacher said to me: 'Go sit down.' At the age of eight I did not know the value of shading. That incident sticks in my mind to this day as my first big flop."*

By the sixth grade Brown had gained some notoriety as a young artist at the Sexton Grammar School. The teachers had him painting murals, posters and anything else requiring artistic talent that came to their minds. He was so busy doing extracurricular activities for the instructors that he flunked the seventh grade. With tears in his eyes he asked his home room teacher why he had not been promoted along with the rest of his class. Following one deep breath and a gulp he blurted the names of a half dozen classmates who he said did not work as hard as he had, but were promoted. The teacher responded: "I expected more of you."

Brown said to the writer: *"In those days what did a Colored kid from a lower class family know about potential? You could not explain to me why I should strive harder and do more to get a back breaking job as a common laborer in the stockyards, steel mills or cleaning somebody's toilet."*

When Buck graduated from Sexton Grammar School in June 1950 he enrolled in the Edward Tilden Technical Vocational School located in a lower middle class white community known as the "Back of the Yards" at 4747 South Union Avenue. He had selected Tilden Tech because he was told he could get a good, solid, technical education there. Tilden was the only school that he had attended where he got the opportunity to use brand new textbooks as opposed to the hand me downs from neighboring white schools. The names of the schools that had originally used the books were always stamped on the front inside of the textbook's hard cover.

The teachers at Tilden were good, but the white boys created a hostile educational environment for Colored stu-

dents. Since Tilden was an all male school the racial con-
frontations were frequently physical. At the suggestion of
the principal Brown and some other Colored students were
transferred to Englewood High School at 6201 South Stewart.
It was a coed school. Brown stated: *"It must have been recess in
heaven because I had never seen so many beautiful Black women in my
life. I started washing under my arms regularly and slicking my hair with
Murray Hair Pomade in an effort to try and look appetizing for those
angels."*

At Englewood High Richard Hunt was the artistic
super star. He was doing unheard of stuff like attending
classes at the Art Institute on Saturdays and studying music
on Friday afternoons at the Abraham Lincoln Center on east
Oakwood Blvd. Buck Brown was 22 years old before he ever
set foot in the Art Institute. Reflecting on his past Buck
Brown states: *"If I had been able to go to a good school with a purpose when I was young and malleable who knows what heights I might
have reached in a true democracy."*

The thought of a Colored person making a living as an
artist never crossed Brown's mind. John Holmes, who
became a Chicago Police Department sketch artist, was a
member of "Buck's" class at Englewood. Holmes went to the
school counselor for guidance. He told the counselor he
wanted to be a commercial artist. The counselor told him he
should choose some other field because he foresaw no future
in commercial art for a Negro. (At the same time that the
school official was giving negative advice to Holmes, E.
Simms Campbell the cartoonist was working for both the
Esquire and New Yorker Magazines in addition to being syndicated nationally in the William Randolph Hearst newspapers. Gordon Parks, author and producer of the movie entitled 'The Learning Tree' was a full time staff photographer for
Life Magazine during the same period.

At age sixteen "Buck Brown" was on his own. His
mother and stepfather decided to move to Detroit where
there were suppose to be better job opportunities. Brown

refused to go to the "Motor City" because he reasoned that things were tough enough in Chicago and in a new city they would be worse. Therefore, he opted to stay in "Abraham Lincoln's City" by the lake. He supported himself during his last two years in high school by bussing dishes at a first class restaurant called the Old Barn on 83rd Street just west of Cicero. In his little red jacket, which was the Old Barn's uniform, he would occasionally be assigned the duty of doorkeeper. The customers had to ring the front doorbell and be buzzed into the establishment's entrance. If the person or persons were not properly attired or looked the slightest bit Jewish or Negroid they were not admitted.

Jerry Kluck and his father Andy were the owners of the Old Barn. Some 20 years later Buck ran across an article in a University Park newspaper about Jerry Kluck who owned the Water Department in the community where the Brown family lived. Buck asked the Village President if that was the same Kluck who used to own a restaurant called the Old Barn. The answer was yes. When the two men finally met at a town hall meeting, they rekindled stories about the Old Barn. Shortly, thereafter Kluck and his wife came by the Browns' home one evening and invited them to have dinner with them at the Old Barn. Everything was the same at the restaurant except the door bell and the buzzer and other restrictive covenants had been removed.

The dinner conversation that evening centered around Buck Brown finishing high school, college and the intervening years that followed. Buck had been fired and rehired by Kluck when he was caught shooting steak bones into a trash can in the fashion of Charlie Brown the DuSable High School basketball super star. Kluck was anxious to hear how his former dishwasher had jumped from the outhouse to the White House in two decades. Buck Brown obliged his host by reciting his odyssey in detail. Brown said:

"When I stepped out into the real world the want ad pages in the daily newspapers were plastered with "Coloreds need not apply" and

174

Some Whites Made Me Feel Like A Five Pound Sack Of Feces

"Whites Only". Westin Armstrong, a friend of mine got me a job packing costume jewelry downtown at Levine's for a dollar an hour.

Christmas was the busy season for costume jewelry. I worked 40 hours overtime. I spent a lot of time figuring out what I was going to do with all of this time and half money I was earning. When payday came around the boss handed me two checks both of them for $40.00. I said, "Hey, wait a minute. Where is my time and a half?" The boss looked at me with a smirk on his lips and said: "What union do you belong to?"

On December 31, 1954, a light bulb went off in Brown's head when he heard a friend talking about joining the Army at a New Year's Eve celebration. He had decided he did not want to continue working at the costume jewelry shop for a $1.00 per hour. He said to his girl friend: *"If I join the Air Force I can kill two birds with one stone in that I can become a military veteran, and also earn entitlement to go to college under the G.I. Bill of Rights. As things stand, I cannot afford to buy you a malted milk shake and take you to the Tivoli Theater to see a movie and stage show."*

On January 12, 1955 Buck Brown became a Buck Airman Basic in the United States Air Force. He was shipped from Chicago to the Lackland Air Base near San Antonio, Texas for basic training. In a very short period, he discovered that integration was a "bitch", the moment a black stepped outside of the allegedly color blind Lackland military reservation.

It was in downtown San Antonio that he and three of his military sidekicks got a racist booty check big time. They were made to feel like a five pound bag of feces. Private Buck Brown described the situation as follows:

"On the Lackland Air Force Base, Negroes could use all facilities including the barber shop without fear of being offended because of their skin tone. However, on this bright and sunny Saturday afternoon we five copper Colored enlisted airmen walked into a drugstore in downtown San Antonio and took adjacent seats at the lunch counter. As we glimpsed the menus, a waitress walked over to us and said, ' I am sorry boys, we don't serve Negroes here, it's a Texas law.' I snapped back, and said, 'Neither do we eat Negroes.' Although that experience is 42 years old the feeling of degradation still floods over my entire body like the waters of

the muddy Mississippi whenever I hear any reference to Texas."

Brown's artistic ability and affability enabled him to sketch life size "Jim Crow" situations about Texas and its people. His cartoons generated cheers rather that jeers. His works kept both white and black servicemen laughing at themselves. His lampoons became so popular that his commanding officer ordered Private Brown to include a caricature of him in his next mural. The cartoons enabled Brown to return to Chicago after being honorably discharged as a non-commissioned officer with an impeccable military record.

As a born again civilian, Brown sustained himself for several years as a bus driver working for the Chicago Transit Authority. He saw and heard such funny material on both the bus and the streets he started carrying a sketchbook and tape recorder to capture both the sights and sounds. As a matter of fact, his C.T.A. superintendent frequently borrowed his sketchbook on weekends, to show to his friends.

Everybody loved Brown's work but nobody was paying him. Brown the artist had been operating on the premise that you had to draw for free in order to get your material in print. Gus Savage, the former Congressman and publisher of the Citizen Community Newspaper opened the commercial door for Brown by offering to buy some of his work.

Brown recalls the following conversation with Savage: *"Gus told me that he was going to pay me $5.00 per drawing. I said Mr. Savage you don't have to pay me anything. Gus said, 'No, no, no, I am going to pay you $5.00 per cartoon.' I drew four caricatures with captions for Gus. He gave me a check for $16.00. I said, 'Gus! Wait a minute. I am not taking math this semester, but the last time I checked 4 x 5 was 20'. That transaction ended with me kissing off $4.00 to the wind."*

Following the Savage episode, Brown started submitting cartoons to the Saturday Evening Post, The New Yorker, and a number of other national magazines. He figured being Black he was going to get turned down, therefore, he opted to

be turned down buy the best. None of the nationally circu-
lated publications gave him the courtesy of a rejection slip.
Such a slip in his opinion would have been an acknowledgement of his existence. The magazines always sent his material back without any comment..

His next port of call was the Chicago based Playboy
Magazine where he asked the receptionist over the phone:
"How do you like for artists to submit cartoons?" She replied: *"8 1/2
x 11 bond paper and a self-addressed envelope."* Brown had seven
ideas but being superstitious, he did not want to send off an
odd number. Therefore, he came up with an eighth drawing
which was a little boy standing in the corner of his bedroom
blowing a trumpet, and facing the wall. His mother and
father were shown peeking through the door. The caption
read: *"No, he hasn't been naughty, he's just imitating Miles Davis."*

Brown lucked out with his eighth drawing. Hugh
Hefner was searching for illustrators for his new show business magazine. Hefner sent Brown a note indicating he was
holding his cartoons for further consideration. Shortly thereafter Buck received a personal note from Hefner suggesting
that he place the little boy with the trumpet further up in the
corner.

On February 4, 1961, Hefner bought the "Little Boy
With The Trumpet" cartoon. Hugh Hefner has continued
buying and copyrighting Brown's work for the past 36 years.

In 1997 there were approximately 125 identifiable
Afro-American cartoonists. Some of the better known ones
including Buck Brown are Robb Armstrong, age 32 and creator of "Jump Start". His works are syndicated by United
Features and appear in 120 daily newspapers.

Los Angeles, gave us Stephen Bentley, 41 who hit the
cartoon Jackpot in 1989 with his "Herb and Jamaal" which
appears in 60 newspapers including the Chicago Tribune, Los
Angeles Daily News and The Seattle Times.

Another winner is Ray Billingsley, 38 of New York City.
His comic strip "Curtis" appears in 200 newspapers across the

country including the Chicago Sun Times, Washington Post and the Detroit Free Press.

Barbara Brandon, 36, the daughter of Brumsi Brandon Jr., creator of "Luther" is opening windows of opportunity for women cartoonists as the first national syndicated Afro-American female cartoonist. Her creation is a strip entitled "Where I'm Coming From". Four decades earlier I recall a female cartoonist named Jackie Ormes who created a comic strip for the Negro owned Pittsburgh Courier.

The Chicago Defender employed more Negro artists than any other publication Black or white, included in that number was Leslie Rogers whose anti-World War I cartoons almost resulted in the Defender being banished from the mail.

Other artists who worked for the Chicago Defender were: Henry Brown, E. Simms Campbell, Jack Chancellor, J.B. Williams, David Ross, Garrett White, C.W. Johnson, Jay Jackson, George Lee, and Chester Commodore, the Defender's editorial cartoonist.

There were thousands of other talented Black artists who never had a chance. Their energies were spent working in the post offices, or walking the 48 states as porters or waiters on the railroad.

CHAPTER 19

AMERICA'S LITTLE CHOCOLATES DON'T MELT

The author's mother, Mittie Travis, affectionately referred to him interchangeably as her sweet little chocolate man or her precious black velvet when he was between the ages of three and five. Those endearing epitchets bathed his psychic with a pleasurably exalted personal image in addition to giving him a very high dose of self esteem. It was not until after he celebrated his 7th birthday that he learned that his mother's little chocolate man could not melt into the American cultural mainstream like boys and girls of other ethnic origins.

His initial culture shock occurred when he and his cousin Frank Hunter presented themselves at the box office of the Oakland Square Theater on Chicago's South Side at 39th and Drexel Blvd. on a Saturday afternoon to see Douglas Fairbanks in Alexandre Dumas' Three Musketeers. The date was on May 19, 1927, when the buxom theater cashier confronted them and said: *"Black boys you cannot come in here.*

Get your 'Nigger' behinds from in front of this theater unless you want them kicked."

The two boys took off for home which was three blocks north of the movie house like two scared rabbits chased by a pack of salivating bloodhounds. Although 70 years have passed, the painful shock of that afternoon is as fresh today as any terrifying experience that might have happened yesterday. The incident forced this writer to become a firm believer in the theory that you may consciously forgive but, subconsciously, you never forget.

The mental scars of racism inflicted upon me during my early years were mere scratches compared to the three gunshot wounds that punctured my body and killed my friend Private Norman Taylor during a racial incident at Camp Shenango in Greenville, Pennsylvania on July 11, 1943.

As opposed to losing blood the following case studies are about individuals whose ego, self esteem, and individuality were scarred.

John London Brown's parents were light-skinned. His mother could pass for a White Anglo Saxon Protestant (WASP), and his father's skin tone was several shades darker than his mother's. If Dr. Johnny Brown, Sr., had chosen to affect a Spanish or Portuguese accent, he could have easily been assimilated into the white world.

Johnny, who was blue-eyed and blond like his mother, never sensed that the world was different for him until he was 6 years old. His awakening came in January 1945, near the end of World War II, when he entered the first grade at the A.O. Sexton Elementary School at 6020 S. Langley in Chicago. When he returned home after his first day in school, his mother asked: *"What color is your teacher? Is she Colored or white"?"*

"What color are we?" Little Johnny queried.

His mother replied, *"We are Colored."*

"The teacher is white," Johnny replied.

Several days later, Johnny's mother visited Sexton

School and discovered that the teacher was as Black as anthracite coal. The little boy's confusion was understandable because he had observed that the teacher's skin color was the opposite of his mother's glistening white face and his own milky white hands. He reasoned that since they were Colored, his teacher must be white.

In the spring of 1947, Johnny's father, an engineer who taught at the University of Chicago, accepted a 4-month assignment in Hawaii. Throughout their ocean voyage, people asked Johnny and his brother Steve what nationality they were. By the second day at sea, the bombardment of questions about race caused Dr. Brown to erupt in anger. He commanded his two young sons to tell anyone who asked them about their nationality that they were Americans.

One elderly lady became a pain in the behind by asking the boys several times a day, *"What race are you?"* On their fourth day at sea, the boys made up something they thought would be incredible enough to squelch her inquisitiveness. They told the lady that they were one sixth Greek, two-sixths Indian, one-twelveth Irish, and every other combination they could think of. The lady did not bother them with her nationality nonsense for the rest of the voyage.

Herb Jeffries, a vocalist with the Duke Ellington Orchestra, had the same experience as the Brown brothers seven years earlier. One night, in September 1940, a patron in a nightclub was sharing a table with a party that included Jeffries. After several rounds of drinks, one member of the party stared at Herb and blurted, *"I assumed you were Colored based on your recordings. But you aren't are you?"*

"What do you mean by Colored?" Jeffries inquired.

"Why, anyone with Negro blood," the man replied.

"Is two drops enough to qualify?" retorted Jeffries.

The man nodded, *"Yes."*

"Negro blood must be some mighty great stuff," the singer recoiled. *"If, for instance, you had a black paint so powerful that two drops of it would turn a bucket of white paint, black that would*

undoubtedly be the most powerful paint in the world."

Jeffries was right about the potency of Black. In the fall of 1955, there was a news wire service story that stated that Black fullback Bobby Grier would sweat, bleed and probably elicit cheers on a Dixie football field. The story upset the people of the sovereign state of Georgia, riled sports circles around the world, and so clouded the mind of then Governor, Marvin Griffin that even his race-baiting henchmen begged him to "grow up."

The young Brown brothers grew and matured so much as first graders that their parents enrolled them in the University of Chicago Laboratory School in the second grade. There was a handful of Black kids in their class plus a thumb and four fingers of Blacks who were one year ahead of them in their new school. Most of the children were sons and daughters of professionals and many, like the Brown brothers, were so light-skinned that they could have passed for white. The brothers knew that 98 percent of the residents in their West Woodlawn neighborhood were Black, and that Hyde Park, was where most of the white students lived. Since their parents had friends among the Black and white races, and all of their father's colleagues at the university were white, the Brown children escaped the full impact of Jim Crow.

When he was in the sixth grade, Johnny was fairly popular among the children at the Lab School. He had lots of white friends, both male and female. At the beginning of the semester in seventh grade, he was invited to attend a dance at the home of a white classmate. That proved to be his last invitation to such an occasion. He later learned that no other Black children had ever been invited to parties given by their white classmates, and it took him a little while to get a fix on what was happening.

Although the Blacks at the Lab School were not invited to any parties, groups of white and Black students would go to the Hyde Park movie theater on Saturday afternoons.

As the tree sap rose in the spring, the students began pairing off into couples. Johnny asked several of the white girls in the group to be his date, but they turned him down. He didn't understand because he was tall, blond, blue-eyed and handsome by WASP standards. Suddenly, a light went on in his head one afternoon when one of the white girls he was pursuing for a date said, *"You will have to talk to my mother."*

Johnny told his mother, who called the girl's mother only to be told that she didn't want her daughter going out with a Colored boy. It was a profound and sobering experience for Johnny Brown when confronted with the fact that although he was popular in the classroom, he could not socialize with the white students after dark. The realization hit him with a bluster more chilling than a 20 degree below zero January wind in Chicago.

Johnny avoided being devoured by hate and anger by associating with a group of white non-athletic, not-too-bright classmates he called misfits. Today, some of them are counted among the avant garde in the professional and business community and are known for not allowing race to become a barrier to friendship. Several of his school mates have become leaders in Fortune 500 companies.

After completing eighth grade, Johnny transferred to Hyde Park High School, where approximately 40 to 50 percent of the students were Black, 40 percent were Jewish and about 5 percent were Japanese. Johnny and his friends referred to Hyde Park as "Zebra Tech" because the students embraced integrated socialization. The choir, the basketball team, the football team and the parties were integrated. White guys were going out with Black girls and Black guys were going out with white girls. The socialization drove their parents nuts. There was no way the Jewish parents could stop their kids from going to Black parties and there was no way that Black parents could stop their kids from going to Jewish parties.

Many of the friendships formed between the Browns

and whites at "Zebra Tech" have survived until this day. When these old friends meet their conversations are laced with talk about the uniqueness of their years at Hyde Park High between 1955 and 1959. They remember when Herbie Hancock, the now-famous pianist/composer, and orchestra leader was elected King of Hyde Park High and thus he became the first Black to attain that lofty status. Hancock's election showed Johnny that there wasn't anything wrong with being Black, and that it was not his fault that he went from a popular person to a pariah at the University of Chicago Lab School. Almost immediately after transferring to Hyde Park High, just three blocks south of the Lab School, Johnny became a popular guy again.

Steve Brown left the Lab School a year after his brother Johnny because he encountered similar racial problems. He had become a reject and punching bag for some of the white toughs. When Steve arrived at Hyde Park High, he rediscovered his outgoing personality and ability to function as a top-flight student, thus mirroring his brother's overnight transformation.

Johnny didn't do too well academically at Hyde Park but he excelled in Popularity 101. For his senior year, his parents sent him to Kushon Academy, Ashburn Anne, Mass., an institution with a reputation for accepting a few Black students, with the purpose of preparing them for a college education.

When Johnny walked into the boys' dorm at Kushon, the 17-year-old Chicagoan didn't know a soul. The dorm was jammed with students engrossed in watching a baseball game on television involving the Milwaukee Braves. It might have been the World Series.

The first words that Johnny heard were, *"Kill that coon!"*

They were talking about Hank Aaron, who was up at bat. Johnny thought, *"Well, if they're gonna kill Hank Aaron on TV, they're gonna kill me now because I'm right at their finger-*

tips." He was terrified. He heard racial references that he had never heard before: like coon, jake, spade, and jungle bunny. *"Oh my God, what is going to happen to me?"* he sighed.

The presence of his first cousin, James, who was lodged across the road in another dorm offered Johnny little comfort because they were the only two Black males in the school. Johnny was scared dungless, a reaction his mother anticipated that he would have in a new environment a thousand miles from home. She had suggested that he take pictures of the family to keep on his dresser for those occasions when someone would come in and ask, *"Well, who are these people?'* Johnny could respond, *"That's my family."*

"Hopefully," his mother said , *"They will get the message and you won't have to explain or wear a sign saying, 'I am a Negro.' "* That proved to be a very effective antidote for countering racial exclusivity.

Although he was at Kushon for just seven months, Johnny was elected the most popular person in his senior class; his cousin James was the second-highest academic achiever in the school's history.

After graduating from Kushon Academy, Johnny went to Grinnell College, in Grinnell, Iowa, which he described as "a piece of cake" because he encountered few racial problems during the four-year tenure. The only glimpse of racism occurred when he was initially assigned to a room with two other Blacks. When his father heard about it, he hit the ceiling and called the president of the college. *"How could a progressive school put three Colored kids in the same room?"* Dr. Brown bellowed.

The boys were immediately switched to different quarters, but after spending one night with their new roommates, they decided they would rather room together. Thus, they became roomies, by choice, for the four years they were at Grinnell.

The college also attempted to match the three Black guys with three Black girls on the campus, but the guys paid the school's match-making efforts very little attention. They dated white as well as Black girls, causing Johnny to describe Grinnell as *"kind of an ideal world."*

Law school proved to be a totally different environment from Johnny's Grinnell experience. He attended Northwestern Law School in Chicago, which he said, *"Was filled with absolute bigots."* There are only two people from his class that Johnny has maintained any communications with today.

Johnny recalls that when he enrolled at the law school, he filled out his application about race and religion honestly, and was assigned a single room at Abbott Hall on the downtown campus off of Lake Shore Drive. Jewish students, were paired off with other Jews or given a single room.

Johnny describes the demographics of the Northwestern law school student body as about one-third Chicago Irish-Catholic, one-third Chicago Jews and one-third WASP from all sections of the country.

Johnny recalls: *They were really a bad group of people.* He said *"The law students were unlike any other students I had known, with their 'We don't like niggers,' attitude. Moreover, during my three years at the law school, they never abandoned their dislike for Blacks. It was a tough place. A lot of the Irish guys were from the Gage Park area on the Southwest Side of Chicago. We're talking about the early '60s, when civil rights issues and Dr. Martin Luther King, Jr. were in the forefront of the news."*

After the end of his first year in law school, Johnny said *"I had swallowed as much of the bigotry as I could stomach without regurgitating green liver bile in the middle of the lecture hall. The situation was so unpleasant that I took every opportunity to leave Abbott Hall for the sanctuary of home with my parents, who had moved from West Woodlawn to Hyde Park."*

Johnny didn't fare very well academically at the law school because he could not concentrate on his studies in that racially charged environment. He told his father that if he didn't drop out, the school would put him out.

Dr. Brown asked, *"Don't you know any members of the faculty? Don't you know any students?"*

Johnny replied, *"I just can't stand it. Dad, you can't imagine how awful it is."* It was a devastating confession for the young man who had been the most popular person in his senior class at the Kushon Academy and was elected class president twice at Grinnell College.

Johnny insisted that he was going to drop out, but his father stomped his foot down on the living room floor and screamed: *"There must be somebody that you can talk to."*

After some thought, Johnny remembered John Kaplan, his professor in a real estate law class. Kaplan was a mild-mannered man who had displayed a real sense of humor. In addition, Kaplan had written a report on desegregating New Rochelle, N.Y., for the Civil Rights Commission on Housing, and Johnny reasoned Kaplan's ethnicity and experience might have given him some empathy for another minority.

Brown was on the mark because Kaplan told Johnny that dropping out of law school would be a big mistake. *"I'm sure you've taken note of the idiots around here,"* he told Johnny. *"These are some of the dumbest people I've ever taught. There is no reason that you can't do the work better than they can. I know that you're smarter than nine-tenths of them, and I'm telling you to stay in school. I will see that the professors in each of your classes give you some attention."*

Johnny moved back into Abbott Hall on North Lake Shore Drive, Kaplan kept his promise and Johnny's grades improved dramatically.

In his third and last year in law school, Johnny Brown assembled a resume that included his activities with the Black Law Students' Alliance.

Johnny recalls his first interview with a major corporation in Detroit. *"I had already been interviewed by two officers of the firm, and things were going great. I felt that I had the job in the bag. A third member of the firm's interview team looked at my resume and came to a dead halt when he reached the section on stu-*

dent activities.   He looked at Johnny and glanced back at the resume several times before continuing the interview."

Brown recalls the following question and answer session:

"Johnny, what is the Black Law Students' Alliance?" the corporate counselor asked.

"It's an organization of Black law students at my law school," Johnny replied.

"Well, I've got a couple of more questions for you," the interviewer said.   "Number one, why do Blacks need an Alliance like this to begin with?"

"It's somewhat of a support group for each of us," Johnny retorted.   "Our law school doesn't have a great number of minority students to begin with.   The Black Law Students' Alliance is kind of a social group and also kind of a close knit support group."

"I don't understand why Blacks would need their own separate group," the lawyer said.

Johnny replied, "For many years Blacks have had to have their separate groups because they weren't allowed in majority groups.   For example, for years the American Bar Association and the Chicago Bar Association did not permit any Blacks to become members."

Johnny had anticipated the next question.   "Why are you in the group?" the corporate counselor asked.

"What do you mean why am I in that group?" Johnny responded.

"I don't understand how you got in the group," the counselor snapped back.

"What do you mean you don't understand how I got in the group?" Johnny retorted.

"Did they have some special type of admissions policy or were you just simply voted in?" queried the corporate counselor.

Johnny decided that he was not going to let the man off the hook.   "I decided I would make him ask me the gnawing question point blank.   Finally, after a group of idiotic questions that you wouldn't expect from a lawyer in a major corporation, he finally asked me the 64,000 dollar question, 'Are you Black?'

"What difference does it make?" Johnny snapped. "Don't you know it's unlawful to ask about race? What is the purpose of that question?"

The counselor softly replied, "I'm just trying to figure out how you got into The Black Students Alliance."

Johnny decided he wasn't going to waste more time playing hide-and-seek on the race issue. "Yes, I am Black," Brown blurted out. "And that's why I'm a member of the organization."

The corporation counselor's face became cherry red. From that point, the interview went downhill.

Johnny said, "I knew when I prepared the resume that if I omitted putting in the fact that I was affiliated with the Black Law Students' Alliance I could have gotten a number of jobs and passed myself off as a white boy. But I have elected not to live a lie." Conversely, Congressman Adam Clayton Powell, D-N.Y., passed for white and joined a white fraternity while a student at Colgate University.

Brown was too culturally Black to be white, and too physically white to be considered Black sans a tag. He felt that his white skin disqualified him from being Black enough to serve as the African American token in a white law firm.

A federal recruiter came to the rescue of Johnny Brown. He was actively recruiting qualified minorities regardless of their sex or the shade of complexion. Thus, Johnny landed his first legal job working for a government body in the District of Columbia. Johnny's white complexion triggered some very interesting experiences during his tour with the U.S. government. One day during a fire drill, a Black secretary ran up to Johnny as he stood in line: *"Do you mind if I ask you a question?"*

Johnny replied, *"Go ahead."*

"There is a rumor going around that you are Black," the secretary said.

Johnny retorted, *"I don't know why there is a rumor going around that I'm Black because I am Black."*

The secretary replied, *"Oh my gosh. They never knew that."*

"What do you mean, they never knew?"

She said, *"I'm certain that most of the lawyers working in this agency don't know that you're Black."*

Johnny could not figure out why the rumor existed— the people that he socialized with during and after work were Black, as were his daily luncheon companions.

All sort of nonsense seeps into the ears of Blacks who appear to be white. For example, when Johnny was trying a case in the state of Washington, a Black witness said, *"The judge is trying to figure out who you are. He knows that you are from Chicago. Beyond that, he doesn't know ethnically what you are and that's causing him a lot of trouble.*

Johnny told the witness:

"I think I understand the judge's problem because almost everyone in the United States from the President to the federal judiciary to Joe and Mary Citizen sitting in the jury box hold a certain personal bias. The bias may focus on age or the sex of an individual. But the overriding prejudice is directed at race. Every individual lawyer, judge or whoever—brings a personal bias into the picture when following a profession or deciding who is going to marry their daughters or sons. That shouldn't be, but it is."

Between 1932 and 1952, more than 5 million light-complexioned Negroes chose to make a complete transformation from the Black world into the white world. During the two decades, thousands more tried living in two worlds, passing as white during the day to find and hold decent paying white-collar jobs and returning to their Negro neighborhoods at night. The dual lifestyles locked them into a Jekyll-Hyde conflict between their day world and their night world. It was a stressful existence to know that some of their white friends would be shocked to learn of their Negro blood and that many of their Negro friends would look upon them with scorn for denying their heritage, despite the fact that they passed for white only to obtain and retain employment.

One girl who passed for white to get work as a clerk in the Marshall Field's department store in Chicago's Loop thought she had lost her job when a well-meaning friend of her mother's came into the store and almost broke her neck doing a double take. *"Well, baby it's sure good to see this store is finally hiring Colored girls,"* she said in a happy surprised voice. Fortunately, the woman was overheard by one person, a white male clerk who was a good friend of the saleswoman and kept her secret.

A young woman, a Harvard graduate who passed in order to hold an administrative position with a large white-owned firm said, *"I'm not ashamed of my race. If I could be Black and still hold this job, I'd let everyone know right now."* Her attitude captured the sentiment of the hundreds of thousands of workers who in 1990 are white by day and Black by night. A 1987 report from the U.S. Bureau of Census indicates the racial crossovers that could occur in the next Century: 100,000 children of mixed parentage were born in the United States in 1987, compared with 30,000 born in 1968. Both of sons of the late Supreme Court Justice Thurgood Marshall are products of a mixed marriage and have crossed over and married white women.

Actress Jennifer Beal was born in Chicago in 1963. Her mother Jeanne is Irish and her Black father Alfred was the prosperous owner of several grocery stores on the south side of Chicago. Alfred died in 1974 and Jeanne, a schoolteacher, moved her family to an all-white North Side community. From that day to the present, Jennifer has never publicly identified with the Black community. In contrast, Jasmine Guy, the female lead in Eddie Murphy's movie "Harlem Nights" and also stared in Bill Cosby's television hit, "A Different World," is the product of a biracial marriage has always presented herself as Black. At the other extreme,

Prince, whose parents were Black, claims in his publicity releases that he is Italian.

America's chocolates don't melt, and neither do marshmallows with chocolate fillings inside.

EPILOGUE

LITTLE ROCK MIRRORS THE AMERICA OF THE 21ST CENTURY

America's 1990s style of racism is a subtle but a fast forwarding attempt to catechise a large segment of the African American community into believing that they are not an under educated and economically disadvantaged people.

Two of the basic components for scaling the Ladder of Success are: Quality education at all levels and equal opportunity upon entry into the labor market. It is self evident that affirmative action and setasides are past due for the years of involuntary servitude, violently forced upon African Americans.

However, as the 20th century ends and the 21st century begins, we find America reverting back to its 19th century mode, in that today we are as separate as the fingers on the hand in resolving the racism issues, in both the job and education arenas.

Among those standing in the vanguard as straw men against filling those educational and economic gaps are some high profile men of color, such as: Supreme Court Justice Clarence Thomas, Thomas Sowell, a senior fellow at the Hoover Institute in California and Ward Connerly, a Sacramento business man and the University of California regent who championed the University's Law against racial preference. Connerly was also Chairman of Proposition 209, a vehicle that bans the use of State of California funds for programs involving race and sex preferences. Texas is in a contest with California in speeding up the banning of racial preferences. In the tenth month of 1997, racial banning is being considered by 20 other states who see the California Law School at Berkeley and the University of Texas at Austin as the laboratories.

In the Fall of 1997, Earl Brooks 27, of Bloomington, Indiana was the only first year law student of color at the University of California at Berkeley. Fourteen other Blacks were accepted at Berkeley but opted to go to other branches of the school in California where they felt that the educational environment would be less hostile.

The number of minority student applicants in the California university system plummeted 26 percent because of anti-affirmative action. To entertain the establishment notion that anti-affirmative action is a safety net for minorities is tantamount to believing that slavery for brothers and sisters, was freedom.

Little Rock celebrated the 40th Anniversary of school desegregation on September 25, 1997. That same day in 1957 the Little Rock Nine under the protection of one thousand members of the 101st Airborne Division and ten thousand federalized Arkansas Guardsmen enforced integration of Little Rock Central High School. The 1997 celebration was found wanting because Little Rock Central High School was in a mode of resegregation. Indeed black and white students now attend the same school but they sit in different classrooms, eat at different tables, sit in different sections at athletic events, and are taught out of different textbooks. The educational condition that prevails in Little Rock, is a mirror of most urban areas in the United States today.

Missing from the event commemorating the 40th year of desegregation at the school were the local and state members and leaders of the NAACP. They boycotted the event because they did not see the 1990s style of neo-segregation as anything to celebrate. However, on hand for President Clinton's address was Daisy Bates, the 1957 NAACP leader and the lightning rod who was in the forefront of the struggle to integrate Little Rock Central High School. Mrs. Bates rose from her wheelchair and waved feebly to the crowd in acknowledgement of the thunderous applause given her when her name was mentioned by one of the speakers.

Mrs. Bates made the following remarks about the Little Rock Nine shortly after they entered the school on September 25, 1957, she said:

The streets were blocked off. The soldiers closed ranks. Neighbors came out and looked. The avenues were full, up and down. Oh! It was beautiful. And the attitude of the children at that moment; the respect they had. Their young faces were saying, 'For the first time in my life I truly feel like an American.' I could see it in their eyes; they knew somebody cared for them - America cared!

President Clinton in his September 25, 1997 remarks on the steps of the Little Rock Central High School where Governor Orval Faubus held court for Jim Crow forty years earlier. Clinton said: *"Segregation is no longer the law, but too often separation is still the rule."*

Throughout their first year at Central High the Little Rock Nine were spat upon and assaulted both physically and verbally. In spite of their ordeals those brave and bright youngsters stayed the course. Today they are all alive and well and living outside of Little Rock with the exception of one. Each morning they answer the roll call in the following places:

Elizabeth Eckford 55, of Little Rock, Arkansas she is unemployed and disabled; she should be remembered forever in a picture that was flashed around the world showing an attractive little Colored girl in a white dress walking alone wearing sunglasses and a serene look on her face as she cradled a notebook in her left arm while surrounded by a white mob taunting her with expletives as she attempted to complete the aborted walk to Little Rock Central High School on September 4, 1957.

Her second effort was on September 25, 1957 when she joined by the balance of the Little Rock Nine, to wit: Melba Patillo Beals, 55, of Sausalito, California, a writer; Ernest Green, 56, of Washington, D.C., managing director of Lehman Brothers Investment Bank; Gloria Ray Karlmark, 54, the Netherlands, a retired lawyer; Carlotta Walls LaNier, 55, of Englewood, Colorado, a real estate broker; Terrence D. Roberts, 55, of Pasadena, California, the Chairman of the Psychology Department at Antioch University; Jefferson Thomas, 56, of Columbus, Ohio, a financial specialist with the Department of Defense; Minnijean Brown Trickey, 56, of Ottawa, Ontario, a social worker; and Thelma Mothershed Wair, 56, Belleville, Illinois, a retired educator.

May the Sun and Moon always shine brightly over their heads and the winds of change blow strongly at their backs.

Dempsey J. Travis
December 11, 1997

A selected amount of material was drawn for this work from the following sources: Interviews, books, newspapers, magazines, journals, newsletter, unpublished papers, scrap books, the author's diaries and personal notes.

INTERVIEWS

Armstrong, Lil Jun 16, 1970.

Armstrong, Louis May 18, 1937.

Anderson, T.J. Mar 11, 1991.

Bell, Carl Feb 16, 1994.

Benedict, Rev. Donald May 5, 1994.

Bonaparte, Jr., William Jan 19, 1991.

Brown, Buck Jul 9, 1997.

Brown, John London Jan 19, 1993.

Bryson, Clemente Feb 28, 1997.

Burris, Roland Apr 19, 1994.

Byrd Jr., Manford May 16, 1994.

Calloway, Cab Jan 14, 1983.

Campbell, Wendell Nov 17, 1991.

Chatman, Linda Nov 6, 1992.

Clark, Walter Apr 18, 1989

Cousins, William Mar 15, 1991..

DeLerma, Dominique Rene Mar 11, 1991.

Dixon, George Apr 21, 1982.

Dickens, Jacoby Apr 22, 1991.

Duster, Benjamin Jan 22, 1997.

Ellington, Mercer Oct 29, 1994.

Finley, Syd May 25, 1994.

Floyd, Samuel Mar 11, 1991.

Grimshaw, Jackie May 20, 1991.

Harriston, Octavia Feb 5, 1991.

Harrston, Glenn M. Feb 22, 1994.

Henderson, Bill Jul 24, 1994.

Hines, Earl Jul 21, 1982.

Hodges, Craig May 9, 1994.

Hunt, Richard Mar 26, 1991.

Jones, Norma E. Feb 13, 1991 and Mar 14, 1991.

King, Paul Jan 23, 1991.

La Fontant, Jewel Jul 23, 1981.

McKinnon, Dennis L. Mar 25, 1994.

Moore, Ralph Feb 14, 1991.

Purnell, Silas Apr 4, 1994.

Pincham, R. Eugene May 7, 1997; Apr 1, 13 and 14, 1997.

Sampson, Rev. Albert Mar 11, 1994.

Smith, Hale Mar 11, 1991.

Stradford, Ernest Jan 14, 1983

Stepto, Robert Feb 20, 1990.

Stewart, Roma Jones Oct 21, 1991; Mar 4, 1996 and Apr 14, 1996.

Tavares, Baldwin Jun 10, 1983.

Taylor, Anita Jan 25, 1991.

Taylor, Hycell B. Mar 11, 1994.

Todd, Thomas N. May 10, 1994.

Wilson, Willie Mar 22, 1994.

Wright Jr., Rev. Jeremiah A. Apr 22, 1991.

Books

Calloway, Cab, and Bryant Rollins, Of Minnie the Moocher and Me, New York: Thomas Y. Crowell Co., 1976.

Chicago Schools: Worst in America, Chicago: The Chicago Tribune Co., 1988.

Giddings, Paula, When and Where I Enter The Impact of Black Women on Race and Sex in America, New York: Bantam Books, 1984.

Jaynes, Gerald David and Robert M. Williams Jr. Eds., A Common Destiny:

Blacks and American Society, Washington, D.C.: National Academy Press, 1989.

Johnson, John H. With Lerone Bennett, Jr., Succeeding Against the Odds, New York: Warner Books Inc. 1989.

Robinson, Jackie, I Never Had It Made, As Told To Alfred Duckett, J.P. Putnam's Sons, New York, 1992.

Travis, Dempsey J., Views From The Back of The Bus During WWII And Beyond, Chicago: Urban Research Press, Inc., 1995.

Travis, Dempsey J., The Duke Ellington Primer, Chicago: Urban Research Press, Inc, 1996.

Travis, Dempsey J., The Louis Armstrong Odyssey: From Jane Alley to America's Jazz Ambassador, Chicago: Urban Research Press, Inc., 1997.

Travis, Dempsey J., An Autobiography of Black Chicago, Chicago: Urban Research Press, Inc.. 1981.

Travis, Dempsey J., Racism: American Style A Corporate Gift, Chicago: Urban Research Press, Inc., 1991.

Travis, Dempsey J., An Autobiography of Black Jazz, Chicago: Urban Research Press, Inc.., 1983.

Travis, Dempsey J., An Autobiography of Black Politics, Chicago: Urban Research Press, Inc., 1987.

Travis, Jack - Editor: African American Architects In Current Practice, Princeton Architectual Press, 1991.

Waters, Enoc P., American Diary- A Personal History of the Black Press,

Chicago: Path Press Inc., 1987.

Young Jr., Whitney M., To Be Equal, McGraw- Hill Book Co., New York, 1964.

Young Jr., Whitney M., Racism: Building A Society. McGraw- Hill, Book Co., New York, 1969.

MAGAZINES

Retired Judge Higginbotham addresses Senate Committee on the need for Affirmative Action, Jet, January 29, 1996.

A Matter of Pride to Reject Racial Kinship is to Embrace Self- hate, by Paul King. Emerge, October 1997.

An Affirmative Retraction Gets A Negative Reaction, Crain Chicago, April 29, 1996.

Art, The Nation ,March 23, 1963.

Combining the root with the reach of Black aspiration. Photo by: Michael Melford - Smithsonian, July, 1990.

Corporate Race War, by Diane Weathers. Essence, Oct. 1997.

Crusaders with pen and ink racially aware Black cartoonists attack social ills with their artistry and wit., by Robb Armstrong. Ebony, January, 1993.

Glass- Ceiling Survival, by Teresa Wiltz. Essence, May 1991.

Negative Action in California: A Gospel Perspective, America, February 22, 1997.

New Racism on Campus, Fortune, February 13, 1989

Picking Up The Pieces - Black

Violence, by Dennis L. Breo. Chicago Tribune, October 18, 1987.

Texaco Case Is Not About Affirmative Action, But Affirmative Opportunity, Crain Chicago, December 2, 1996.

The Rodney King Case reaffirmed black distrust of the courts, and statistical evidence indeed suggests that race bias unbalances the scales of justice, by Lynn Duke. Emerge, December, 1992.

The Myth of Meritocracy Opinion: Why Do Racial Preferences Get Us So Steamed, by Ellis Cose. Newsweek, April 1995.

Wisdom Bridges, a public sculpture by well-known Chicago artist, Richard Hunt. Photo: Kathryn Kolb - Art Papers/Jan/Feb. 1991.

NEWSPAPERS

40 Years Later Women Heal Racial Scars in Little Rock. Chicago Sun-Times, September 24, 1997.

40 Years, Still Healing. Chicago Tribune, September 26, 1997.

700 Urge Ouster of Rutgers Leaders, by Donna de La Cruz. Chicago Sun-Times, February 2, 1995.

A Reverse Discrimination Suit Shatters Two Teachers' Lives, by Brett Pulley. New York Times, August 3, 1997.

After Little Rock, a New Resegregation, by Clarence Page. Chicago Tribune, September 28, 1997.

Architect, Urban Planner. - Wendell J. Campbell.

Beyond Jazz and Rap. Southtown Economist, September 10, 1992.

Black or White? Labels Don't Always Fit, by Michael Eric Dyson. New York Times, February 13, 1994.

Black America's Quiet Chasm African Americans at Odds with Caribbean Immigrants, by Sam Fulwood III.. Chicago Sun-Times.

Black Maestros on the Podiums, But No Pedestal, by Robert Schwarz. New York Times, October 11, 1992.

Black and Cuban-Americans: Bias in Two Worlds. New York Times, September 13, 1997.

Black Composers Seek to Emerge as a Force in Classical Music, by Edward Rothstein. New York Times, April 14, 1994.

Black Music Ensemble Shows Rich Range, by Howard Reich. Chicago Tribune, April 5, 1994.

Black Pioneer's Life Delivers a Message for Conductors Today, by Mary J. Alexander. Chicago Sun-Times, February 21, 1993.

Climbing the Scale/Orchestras Adjusting Slowly to Concept of Racial Balance, by Wynne Dalacoma. Chicago Sun-Times, January 17, 1995.

Constructing Inroads for Future Black Architects, by Cordie Watson. Chicago Defender, June 9, 1984.

Corporate America's Wake-Up Call, by Laura S. Washington. Chicago Tribune, December 12, 1996.

CSO, Lyric Plan Adds to Reality Shock. by

Vernon Jarrett. Chicago Sun-Times, March 7, 1993.

CSO's Morgan Helps Open Way for Blacks, by Lori Rotenberk. Chicago Sun-Times, November 1, 1992.

Deposition: Avis Knew of Complaints. USA Today, November 14, 1996.

End to Racial Policy Could Hurt University of California, Panetta Warns. Chicago Sun-Times, July 24, 1995.

Ex-Exec Charged in Texaco Bias Case. Chicago Tribune, November 20, 1996. Tribune News Service.

Ex-Texaco Official Charged with Obstruction of Justice, by Kurt Eichenwald. New York Times.

External Factors Responsible for Lack of Black Musicians, by Wynne Delacoma. Chicago Sun-Times, March 14, 1992.

Folk Art or Racial Stereotypes? Vintage Films Remain Problematic, by Donald Liebenson. Chicago Tribune, September 18, 1997.

Glass Ceiling Cited by Black Bank Officers. Chicago Tribune, December 20, 1997.

Group Rallies to Support Blacks in Classical Music, by Theresa Cameron. Chicago Sun-Times, August 4, 1991.

Henry Lewis First Black Conductor at New York Met. Chicago Sun-Times, January 29, 1996.

Hunter-Gault Hits the Glass Ceiling, by Howard Rosenberg. Chicago Sun-Times, August 7, 1994.

In Little Rock, Clinton Warns of Racial Split. New York Times, September 26, 1997.

Justice For All? Legal System Struggles to Reflect Diversity, But Progress is Slow, by Ellen J. Pollack, Stephen J. Adler. Wall Street Journal, May 8, 1992.

Lone Black in Law Class Fights End of Preferences, by Dion Hayes. Chicago Tribune, September 29, 1997.

Musician with a Mission: Conductor Michael Morgan Orchestrates New Levels of Understanding, by John Von Rhein. Chicago Tribune, May 16, 1993.

New Start for Chicago Capital Fund Project. Crain Chicago Business, April 8, 1991.

Northern Trust Denies Scrubbing Mortgage Files, by John Schmeltzer. Chicago Tribune, November 10, 1996.

Offensive Report Leads to Shake-Up, by Michelle Roberts. Chicago Sun-Times, September 18, 1997.

On Once Liberal Campuses, Racial Divide Grows Wider. New York Times, October 25, 1995.

Progress Stumbling on Road from Little Rock., by Carl Rowan. Chicago Sun-Times, September 28, 1997.

Pushing Mail Carts on the Road to Power at William Morris, by Monique P. Yazigi. New York Times, May 23, 1994.

Questions of Race Run Deep for Foe of Preferences, by Barry Bearak. New York Times, July 27, 1997.

Racism Not Issue Busing Foes Say, by Raymond Coffey. Chicago Sun-Times, August 26, 1994.

Remembering the Great Victory of Little Rock Nine. Chicago Defender, October

4, 1997.

Renewed Hope for Black Architects, by Eve M. Kahn. New York Times.

Richard Hunt Fashioning Metal to Life. N'Digo Magazine, September 24, 1997.

Rutgers Chief Denies Intending to Link Heredity and Test Scores, by Jon Nordheimer. New York Times, February 2, 1995.

Rutgers President says He Didn't Mean Remarks on Heredity (Associated Press). Chicago Tribune, January 1, 1995.

Sculptor Richard Hunt: Even His Trash is Art, by Adrienne Drell. Chicago Sun-Times, November 27, 1994.

Segregation Apology Sought from Clinton, by Sonya Ross. Chicago Sun-Times, September 30, 1997. Associated Press.

Sinfonietta Provides Sounding Board for Black Composers, by Frederick H. Lowe. Chicago Sun-Times, January 15, 1995.

Some Old Stereotypes - Myths About Elderly Twist Public Opinion. Chicago Sun-Times, November 1, 1992.

Standard Tests for College Under Fire in Diversity Debate, by Karen Brandon. Chicago Tribune, September 28, 1997.

Suit Accuses Donnelley of Racial Bias. Chicago Sun-Times, November 26, 1996.

Testing the Waters, Dropping the SAT Would Mean Failing Students, by Stephan Chapman. Chicago Tribune, October 10, 1997.

Texaco Tapes Show Bias in Workplace Far from Gone. USA Today, November 14, 1996.

Texaco Suit Settled for $176 Million, by Jim Fitzgerald. Chicago Sun-Times, November 16, 1996.

Texaco Executives, on Tape, Discussed Impeding a Bias Suit, by Kurt Eichenwald. New York Times, November 4, 1996.

Texaco Calls Woes 'Tip of Iceberg'. Chicago Sun-Times, November 18, 1996. Associated Press.

The State of Race Relations in Black and White, by Clarence Page. Chicago Tribune, September 17, 1997.

The Identity Myth, by Richard Sennett. New York Times, January 30, 1994.

The Undoing of a Diva: Why Here? - Edward Rothstein. February 27, 1994.

The Right Call - Telecommunications Whiz Hooks Up a Great Career, by Ingrid E. Bridges. Chicago Defender, April 10, 1995.

The Greening of America's Black Middle Class. New York Times, June 18, 1995.

The Man With 20-20 Vision, by Joy Darrow. Chicago Defender, December 16, 1974.

The Two Faces of Texaco, by Kurt Eichenwald. New York Times, November 10, 1996.

Three Black Artists Tell Forum of Their Pains and Gain, by Howard Reich. Chicago Tribune, February 28, 1991.

Time Uncovers Discrimination. East Chicago Heights Times, October 8,

1995.

Truth Will Set Us Free - But the Lie Won't
Allow It, by Thomas Sowell. Chicago
Sun-Times, September 30, 1997.

Two Marian Andersons, Both Real, by
David Mermelstein. New York Times,
February 23, 1997.

Ulysses Kay Prolific American Composer.
News Service, New York Times, May 28,
1995.

University of Michigan Sued Over
Diversity. Associated Press, Sun-Times,
October 15, 1997.

Why Does the Majority of White America
Fear Black Males? The Hampton
Roads, January 4-10, 1997.

William Grant Still: Outstanding
Composer, by Tara Y. Locke. Chicago
Defender, March 9, 1993.

Wynton Bites Back: Addresses His
Critics, by Willard Jenkins. National
Jazz Org., 1994.

JOURNALS

A History of Local 208 and the Struggle
for Racial Equality in the American
Federation of Musicians, by Clark
Halker. Black Music Research Journal,
Vol. 8, Fall, 1988.

Opening Doors In Music. - Benjamin J.
Novak.

The African-American Music Tree Study
Guide - The Corporation for Public
Broadcasting. South Carolina
Education Radio, WQED-FM,
Pittsburgh. Public Radio International,
Fall, 1988.

Index

Index

Brown, Doris (Mother) - 170-171

Brown, Henry - 178

Brown, Howard (Stepbrother) - 170

Brown, Irving (Brother) - 170, 171

Brown, John London - 181

Brown, Michael "Fate" (Father) - 170

Brown, Sr. Johnny - 181

Brown, Wayman (Stepbrother)

Brown, William - 30

Bryson, Clemente - VI, 43-48

Buckingham Fountain, Chicago, IL - 59

Builders Association of Greater Chicago
    (BAGC) - 68

Burnett, Robert - 77

Butler, Arthur - 2

California Law School at Berkeley, CA -
    195

Calloway, Cab -151-160

Calloway, Nathaniel (Dr.) - 126, 127

Calumet High School, Chicago, IL - 58

Camp Shenango, PA - 181

Campbell, E. Simms - 173, 178

Campbell, Herman W. (Father) - 22

Campbell, Leroy - 30

Campbell, Selma Smith (Mother) - 23

Campbell, Wendell - V, 21-30

Cape Giradau, Missouri - 107

Carbondale Community High School - 106

Carbondale, IL - 5, 106

Carter, Aida Arabella (Mother) - 140

Carter, Jimmy (Pres.) - 16, 42

Carver, George W. - 98

Central H.S., Little Rock, AR - 195-197

Champaign, Illinois - 107, 122, 157

Chancellor, Jack - 178

Chase, John 30

Chase Manhattan Bank , N.Y.- 117

Chase Western Reserve University (Ohio)
    - 12

Chatham Area, Chicago, IL - 72, 74

Chatman, Linda C. - IV, 165-168

Chemical Bank, New York , N.Y.- 67

Chicago Art Institute - 96, 99,
    100, 101, 173

Chicago Bar Association - 142, 189

Chicago Board of Trade (C.B.O.T.) - 9

Chicago Capital Fund - 66

Chicago City Colleges - 74

Chicago Colored Y.M.C.A. - 83

Chicago Defender - 12, 13, 178

Chicago Housing Authority - 108

Chicago, Illinois - 16, 22, 25, 34, 36, 51-
    53, 59, 77, 88, 97, 140

Chicago Loop - 65, 67, 192

Chicago Lying-In Hospital - 123

Chicago Police Dept. - 173

Chicago Post Office - 4

Chicago Public Schools -
    59, 67, 85, 96, 144

Chicago River - 53

Chicago Stockyards - 124, 134

Chicago Sun-Times - 168, 178

Chicago Transit Authority - 176

Chicago Tribune - 177

Chicago Urban League - 108, 127

Children's Memorial Hospital, Chicago, IL
    - 83

Cincinnati Art Museum - 101

Cincinnati, Ohio - 22, 23

Circuit Court of Cook County, IL - 86

Citizen Community Newspaper - 176

Civil Rights Commission on Housing -
    16, 188

Civil Service - 14, 15, 17

Civil War - 55, 81

205

Index

Index

Index

Index

Index

Index

Moore, William Jr. (Brother) - 4

Morehouse University, Atlanta, GA - 56, 67

Morgan, Garrett - 98

Morgan State University (Maryland) - 18

Morris, Edward H. - 12

Morris, Robert (Dr.) - 127

Morris, Sydney - 25- 27, 28

Morrison, Tennessee - 170

Morrison, William - 25

Mt. Sinai Hospital, Chicago, IL - 130, 131, 132

Murphy, Eddie - 193

Museum of the Twentieth Century, Vienna - 101

NAACP - 13, 143, 146, 153, 195, 196

Nash, Diane - 13

Nashville Grand Ole Opry - 45

Nashville, Tennessee - 13, 45, 46, 75- 77

National Association of Minority Contractors - 30

National Bar Association - 142, 149

National Gallery, Washington DC - 101

National Honor Society - 24

National Museum of Israel, Jerusalem - 101

National Museum of American Art, Washington, DC - 101

National Negro Congress - 143

National Organization of Min. Arch (NOMA) - 30

National Scholarship Foundation - 76

National Urban League - 29

Nelson- Atkins Museum of Art, Kansas City - 101

New Bonaparte Corp. - 67

New Jersey, New Jersey - 65

New Jersey State Museum, Trenton, NJ - 101

New Orleans, Louisiana - 81

New Orleans, Louisiana - 158

New York City College, N.Y. - 40

New York, New York - 24, 29, 67, 100, 141, 154, 164

New Yorker Magazine - 173, 176

Nixon, Richard - 144

Northwestern University - VIII, 2, 3, 8, 13, 46, 47, 85, 121, 122, 123, 187

Oakland Square Theater, Chicago, IL - 180

Oberlin College, Ohio - 140, 145

Oglivie, Gov. Richard - 149

Old Barn Restaurant, Chicago, IL - 174

Operation Push, Chicago, IL - 6

Ormes, Jackie - 178

Ottawa, Ontario - 197

O'Hare, George - 63, 64

Palm Springs, California - 54

Palmer House, Chicago, IL - 84

Pantry Pride - 147

Parks, Gordon - 173

Partee, Cecil (Attorney) - 85

Pasadena, California - 197

Patillo, Melba - 197

Paul Robeson Glee Club - 24

Payne, Dr. Helen - 3, 121

Peabody Hotel, Memphis, TN - 83, 84

Pearl Harbor - 83, 171

Penn, Ralph (Dr.) - 2

Pennsylvania State College - 38, 39

Petrowski, Danny - 62

Phi Beta Kappa - 13

Philadelphia, Pennsylvania - 38, 67

Index

Index

Index

Index

Walker, Madame C.J. - 98

Washington, DC - 13, 30, 101, 129, 131

Washington, Harold - 65, 85

Washington Park, Chicago, IL - 171

Washington Park Court, Chicago, IL -
140

Webster, Milton - 142

Weir, Miss. - 4

Wendell Campbell Associates - 29

West Chesterfield Community, Chicago,
IL - 58

West Palm Beach, FL - 154

West Woodlawn Area, Chicago, IL - 121

West Woodlawn Community, Chicago, IL
- 121, 183

Western Freedmen's Aid Commission - 13

WFM-TV, Nashville, TN - 45, 46

Wharton School of Finance, Philadelphia,
PA - 67

Wheeler, Lloyd G. - 20

White, Charles - 96

White, Garrett - 178

Whitney Museum of American Art, New
York - 101

Wilberforce, OH - 106

Wilberforce University, OH - 106

Willard Elementary School, Chicago, IL -
144

Williams, Daniel Hale - 12, 131

Williams, Harold

Williams, J.B. - 178

Williams, James - 7

Williams, Joe - 171

Williams, Paul Revere - 26, 29

Willis, Benjamin C. - 58, 59

Wilson, Arthur J. - 9

Wilson, Bob - 30

Wilson Company, Chicago, IL - 134

Wilson, Henry I. (Dr.) - 126

Wilson Junior College, Chicago, IL - 73

Wilson, Teddy - 154

WKOA-TV, Denver, CO - 40

Woodlawn Hospital, Chicago, IL - 130

World War I - 178

World War II -
23, 51, 75, 83, 135, 161, 172, 181

WPA (Work Progress Administration) -
170

Wright, Edward H. - 12

Wright, Roy - 83

Wright, W.T. - 82, 83

Yale University - 135

Young, Jr., Whitney M. - 29

Zenith Corporation - 47

"Back of the Yards", Chicago, IL -
124, 134, 172

"City of Brotherly Love" - 39

"Everyday I Have the Blues" - 171

"Old Boys Network" - 35

"Sleepy Time Down South" - 158